AS SEEN ON TV

BY THE SAME AUTHOR

AUTOBIOGRAPHY OF A FACE

AS SEEN ON TV

PROVOCATIONS

LUCY GREALY

BLOOMSBURY

Copyright © 2000 by Lucy Grealy

All rights reserved. No part of this book may be used
or reproduced in any manner whatsoever without written permission
from the Publisher except in the case of brief quotations embodied
in critical articles or reviews. For information address
Bloomsbury, 175 Fifth Avenue, New York, NY 10010.

Published by Bloomsbury, New York and London.

Distributed to the trade by St. Martin's Press.

Library of Congress Cataloging-in-Publication Data
has been applied for

ISBN 1–58234–153–2

First published in the U.S. by Bloomsbury in 2000
This paperback edition published 2001

10 9 8 7 6 5 4 3 2 1

Typeset by Hewer Text Ltd, Edinburgh
Printed in the United States of America by
R.R. Donnelley & Sons Company, Harrisonburg, Virginia

CONTENTS

YOU ARE HERE; A MAP TO THIS BOOK

SOMETIME AROUND MY JUNIOR year in college, a year when I was particularly earnest in my desire to know the meaning of life, and a year when I had just enough education behind me so as to inform and direct but not yet temper or tamp my zeal, it occurred to me that rather than spend my time trying to find the answers, it might be more worthwhile, or at least worth the change in scenery, to focus on the questions themselves. I'd been reading a book on theoretical mathematics (don't let that fool you; I can barely add and subtract and I can't multiply past 3×7; reading books on theoretical mathematics is my way of overcompensating), and for the first time I understood the abstract meaning of an equation; the information on both sides of the equal sign are *equal*. Of course the concrete aspect of this had been unsuccessfully forced upon me for years, so much so that the abstract meaning of it eluded me until this one particular day while reading in the college coffee house. Before, equations, particularly algebraic equations, had seemed a torture of the Inquisition genre, where the assumption was that simple terror and complex physical suffering would uncover the truth. All equations were, mostly, about how stupid I was, and the journey from one side of an equal sign to the other, from $3n$ to 15, from the question to the answer, was a deeply murky crossing completed successfully only by blind groping and luck.

But the sudden simple truth of the matter, that in essence and in fact the answer was already present, startled me. I had to look up from my book at the others sitting innocently around me and wonder if I should go tap someone on the shoulder and ask if it was true; you mean that the information on one side of an equal sign is the same as what is on the other side of an equal sign, but stated in a different form? I'd always been so linear about it before, thinking in terms of an exacting narrative, a process of answering Sphinx-like questions that made no sense. To see an equation as a whole unit, however, was a uniquely different experience; it was no longer a progressive mystery, but a sublime statement about how the question and the answer are distinguishable from each other only by form, that 15 *is* 3n; the same thing said in different ways. Before, my questions about life were like large bowls I filled as best I could with fragmented answers I picked up along the way. Now, however, life itself *was* the answer, and my job, as I saw it, was to start finding the questions worthy of it, equal to it. The obtuseness of my repeated verbal pleas with the universe to surrender its meaning became immediately apparent; of course there is no grammatically correct answer, or logical answer, or even a purely emotional one.

Martin Heidegger, in *What Is Thinking?*, suggests that intelligence, rather than being the assertion of what is known, is like an arrow piercing continuously into the unknown, and that it can only be of value when treated as something that provides us with ever greater stores of ignorance. Jacques Lacan also felt (along with many poets and mystics) that the 'real' is what cannot be said, and that our apparent selves are simply the detritus of what we do say. In Thomas Mann's *The Magic Mountain*, Hans Castorp says he would rather risk sounding bumbling and foolish while trying to say a true thing than to sound smart while speaking in well-ordered platitudes.

These essays are the leftover evidence of my asking questions in various forms, and I also like to think of the essays as questions themselves, questions that focus on trying to perceive and experience the already present answer, life itself, as openly as possible. Necessarily, because it's impossible to occupy all possible forms at once (is that what enlightenment is?) the forms here vary widely. I wanted to know what I would find if I asked my questions in a very prescribed, precise way, as well as what is to be found from letting sentences open up and wander, as well as what is created when disparate topics are layered one upon the other.

Many of these essays were written at the request of anthology editors, all of whom allowed me great leeway; some are the twisted results of magazine editors' requests and were written for money, though most of my magazine pieces get killed because I get carried away and then can't bring myself to neuter the results; and many of these essays I wrote simply for the pleasure of the act. Though the accents in which these questions are asked span the frontal lobe, it's my hope that the voice they are asked in remains, if nothing else, and even when foolish and sputtering, earnest.

AS SEEN ON TV

SO, FOR REASONS THAT will become obvious, I've changed a few identifying details in the following anecdote. It all started with my sitting at home feeling ignored one afternoon, when the phone rang. It was a producer at a certain daytime talk show. I don't watch daytime talk shows with any regularity – I don't actually watch TV with any regularity because I don't have cable which means, in Manhattan, that I don't have any reception. When I do get near a TV – in hotels, when I visit my mother, when I visit my friend Stephen's house – I watch it with great hunger and amusement. The so-called real shows are my favorites, like that one where people with gunshot wounds and pit bull bites and knives in their heads get rolled into various ER rooms around the country; or that I-just-happened-to-have-my-camcorder-on show in which planes crash into the audiences at military air shows and circus elephants run amok and toss innocent bystanders into the air, or actually, come to think of it, not-so-innocent bystanders because they were participating in the public humiliation of the elephant by watching it in a circus and thought that this culturally imperial activity of parading around interesting 'things' from the provinces for their own amusement was suitable entertainment for their kids, and come to think of it those people at the airshow, I mean, what kind of entertainment is that, showing your kids how glorified it is to fly a military plane whose original purpose it is to kill people anyway and then thinking it's a big tragedy when they crash into the audience and kill people, even though those weren't the actual dead people the designers of the plane had in mind; or that show which I don't really like but watch anyway because sometimes it's the only 'real' thing on, that show about the cops.

But daytime talk shows; no, I'm sorry, I just can't watch those no matter how desperate for TV I may get. The level of reality channeled there is just too depressing, the reality of what a big bunch of losers we all are. But my disdain of daytime talk shows doesn't mean I don't *know* about the various daytime talk shows. Stephen, for instance, watches them with great relish, and sometimes I am, well, sort of forced (my word) into watching them. And James, this guy I used to go out with, he loved them too, and I kept finding myself, on dates, having to discuss issues that had been aired on these shows. All of the issues, it seems, concern interpersonal relationships, and are about the various ways in which we cheat on, are turned on by, don't understand, are misunderstood by, and generally don't get on with but are willing to be, after being long lost from, reunited with each other. Though I've heard rumors that some of the 'better' talk shows tackle (their word) important issues, I have yet to actually see this happen. Or maybe the issues *are* important; just because I don't want to sleep with obese people and have hurt my obese mother's feelings because I don't want to sleep with obese people doesn't mean that, if I were to parse the situation carefully enough, there isn't an important issue being presented.

So, though I had never watched the show the producer who called me produced, I had seen enough *Today on X we will be discussing* X promo spots to have a sense of the show. I had the vague recollection that it was one of the 'important' shows that tackled 'big' issues. The issue *du jour* was physical suffering, how people were able to survive and come out better people for having gone through some form of horrendous physical suffering. Now, not *my* physical suffering; no, the producer (a woman, perky sounding, young, blond, and skinny sounding) didn't want me to talk about my own physical suffering, something I'd already talked about *ad nauseam* on my very own number of talk shows (though never this particular talk show) in a deluded effort to sell my book to all those serious readers out in the audience. No, this show was about other people telling their own horrendous suffering stories, and this one guest, *my* guest, one of six guests (the other guests had suffered horrendously because of things like, though not exactly like, being crashed into at military air shows and gored by righteously outraged elephants), his horrendous suffering was that some nut had kidnapped him, tortured him, and then tried to bury him alive. It sounded like a nightmare, even just in that one short sentence. And after it was all over, while he was recuperating in the hospital, he happened to read my book about my own horrendous physical suffering and now I was his hero. I was such a hero and he was such a vocal fan about how I was his hero that the producer called me up and asked if I would secretly come on the show to surprise him. After all, she pointed out, he's been through so much. It'll be a beautiful moment, she said.

So, because I am a good person and because I was in an I-don't-get-enough-attention mood, I agreed and the next morning a limo was waiting for me outside my apartment. This was unfortunate because my landlord happened to see me getting into the limo and it just so happened I was late with my rent. Even though it was obviously not *my* limo, the very act of getting into a limo in order to be delivered to a TV studio doesn't jibe with the matter of one's rent being late. Any jury would convict me based on the evidence. Ever since I'd been on TV all of my friends – and my landlord and the student-loan people and my brother – thought I was rich and that I should give them money, and I'd discovered it was tiring and fruitless to explain the reality of how, even though I was an author who'd been on TV, all that meant was that I earned as much money as any low- to mid-level secretary *without* the medical benefits or retirement fund or paid sick days or the pretense of job-security or the interesting possibility of being sexually harassed. The only thing that made the limo remotely OK was that it was actually a *super stretch* limo, which meant that we, well, I mean, he, Angelo, my limo driver, who later on the way home asked me out on a date but I turned him down because I was still freaked out over what I haven't told you about yet, had to take turns *really* wide and so block Midtown traffic. This gave people a much-welcomed excuse to honk their horns and glare righteously at us, all of which pointed to the fact that the limo was so long as to be ridiculous, and I tend to think the act of being ridiculous is by itself a redeeming act, except, of course in the cases of military airplane pilots, congress, and people who refuse to spay/neuter their pets (and don't think I don't know these activities overlap).

Limos used to be sure signs of celebrity, but now they are just crass. The truth is, I thought they were crass even when they were sure signs of celebrity, but no one was listening to me back then. Doctoral students in cultural theory and cultural criticism programs around the world have written many a thesis on the limo, its tangled web of signifier and significants. They've also written many a thesis and many an article (whole books in fact) on daytime talk shows. I have to confess something here; I love reading cultural criticism. I think it is very entertaining, and since I don't watch TV, I think I deserve a little entertainment now and then. My friends think I am nuts; they don't understand why someone would willingly read books with sentences like 'Ultimately, the surface meaning system means that the system of veneration, the process of succession of valued human identities, is more important than what anyone individual may represent.' They just don't get what a hoot that sentence is, how much it tickles me, and at the same time they don't get how incredibly tender and meaningful I find our pretentious and idiotic attempts to sound like we know what we're talking about. Take this essay for example, the one I'm writing right now and the one you'll be reading in another now; I mean, I started the whole essay with the word *So*, and since then I've been relentlessly vernacular, interrupting myself and going off on tangents and including extraneous information, all of which makes this essay the embodiment of exactly what I was taught *not* to write in high school. Back then, it was all about making a statement and then supporting it, about trying to sound smart, like you knew what you were doing, what you were thinking, what was important and why. Ha. The original purpose behind the early cultural critics (German and East European intellectuals that came to America after they got booted out of or voluntarily left Fascist World War II Europe) was that even while they were using the most smart-sounding (or dumb-sounding, depending on your stance) language to explain themselves, what they were actually trying to say was not just how *meaningless* such formal structures were (the idea of how an essay should be written, for instance) but that the true meaning of such structures were hidden, and that the 'true' meaning often lay in *how* the meaning was hidden. You might think it's a good idea to write a formal essay and sound smart, and it's not a bad place to start from, but what's also happening is that you're being taught the value of neat, containable ideas, which is a total sham because the truly interesting (and radical) ideas are usually rather sloppy and run-on, and unless you learn (and no one is going to teach you this) how to be sloppy and run-on in a genuinely honest and productive way (which is almost impossible, let me tell you), then you can only continue to interact with the 'structures' (whether it's an essay or a limo) in a way that's never going to get beyond the popularly accepted meaning of them, which, if you believe these guys, is a false meaning anyway (false in that the accepted meaning – like that the best essays are neat essays – pretends to be the whole truth when it's actually only a part of the truth, which is worse than being openly false), and it's also exactly what the so-called power structure would like you to keep on doing, because if you don't get beyond the initial meaning of a form or structure you can't question it, or challenge it, in any serious way. It's intensely political stuff, and all about power: who has it and how they get to keep it. It's not just who gets to be driven around in the limo and why, but why we care in the first place, and why we think getting into a limo and going on TV means that you should have enough money to pay your rent on time.

A big problem I used to have with ideas like this is that they sounded so Dr Evil, that there was this 'they' who were living in a bunker in Colorado and planning to dupe us in all these elaborate ways involving Mr London (my high school English teacher: Hi, Mr London!) and daytime talk shows, and that the CEOs of advertising and oil companies were all very dastardly and got together once a year to drink martinis and laugh at our childlike ways while plotting yet more genius control mechanisms like the Oscars, Air Jordans, and *Married with Children*. Since then I've learned it's even more insidious than this, that while those at the top are claiming they have our best interests at heart when they cut that spending and abolish those rights, that rather than lying, which is what I used to think they all did, I've come to realize they actually *believe* they have our best interests at heart, that they are doing the right thing. There is no clear *hierarchy* here with a Dr Evil at the top and a band of loyal little dr evils carrying out his orders, but rather the very *system* of power is organic and alive and self-sustaining, just like any other neurosis. People don't necessarily plan to pull the wool over other people's eyes (well, sometimes they do) but they do find themselves in places of privilege and power and then go about unconsciously justifying their positions; it's a very human thing to do as an individual, and the culture we create as a collection of individuals around such justifications is very successful in that it continues not to just survive, but to flourish.

So, anyway, back inside the limo. Well, actually, I'm out of the limo now. Now I'm at the studio, which is in a surprisingly decrepit building not far from Times Square. I like my TV studios to be like my hospitals and kitchens and bathrooms: gleamingly new and full of amenities. This place was falling apart; the carpets, not pretty to begin with, were stained, and the ceiling had a number of interesting holes. Worse, because I was a 'surprise' guest and couldn't go in the real green room for obvious reasons, I had to settle for a conference room with uncomfortable chairs, not enough heat, no monitor to watch what was being recorded on stage, and no coffee (most green rooms usually have at least some coffee with powdered kreme and a phone and couch or something; keep the talent happy, you know). Young interns kept coming into my large but desolate conference room and asking me earnestly if I wanted anything. 'Water, I'd love some water.' 'I'll get you some,' and they'd walk out and I'd never see them again. Half an hour later, another intern would walk in and we'd go through the dialogue again; I was there for over two hours and I never did get any water. I felt sort of neglected. (The previous statement is either a symptom of incipient prima donna syndrome, or I was just really thirsty; I can't remember the actual connotations now.)

After enough neglect, I decided to go for a walk through the decrepit and strangely empty offices of the daytime talk show. I was a little disappointed by the whole green room thing, and also this strange vacuous time I seemed to be expected to fill all by myself. Most shows don't give you a whole lot of hanging-out time. On the *Today* show I had just enough time to drink one cup of coffee, go to makeup, then get to the set and realize I had to urinate from the coffee. Luckily, I've learned, once the camera goes on you magically forget you have to urinate, though I did once pass gas on CNN (I don't think the microphone picked it up.) Along with me in the green room of the *Today* show was this guy I couldn't quite place, though I knew I knew him. He got called to the set before me and the next thing, there he was on the monitor, and instantly, in the quotation marks of the TV set, swaddled in the context of broadcast, I recognized him as the famous lead singer of a rock band.

Another time I walked into another green room in a different city and this woman I sort of recognized saw me, stood up with a big smile and said, 'Lucy! I'm sooo happy to meet you.' It turned out to be a famous writer who'd read my book and felt she knew me, and since she was a famous writer (though I hadn't actually read her work) I sort of felt I knew her, too. We had a great time in the green room, yakking it up like old friends, and promised to see each other again in our home city. Later, on the plane, I was in that half-asleep plane state I adopt to forget I'm on a plane, and I was musing abstractedly about my good buddy, this famous writer, when suddenly I realized I didn't actually know her from Adam, that she was not, in fact, my good buddy, nor I hers. I tried to trace this feeling back to its roots, and I realized it was the look she gave me when I walked into the room; it was a look of recognition. Since then, I've done some experiments, experiments that are particularly fruitful to conduct on the streets of New York. The experiment is this:

Look at people you pass, strangers, as if you recognize them. Try it; it's amazing. You can look at people on the street with lust, disgust, desire, horror, shock, all kinds of looks, and people in New York won't even glance at you. But look at someone as if you suddenly recognize them and it disarms them utterly; they can't *not* not deal with your looking at them like that. Human to human. Two animals of the same species *seeing* each other.

As I was wandering the halls of the daytime talk show (I felt like I was doing something *verboten*; didn't I at least need a hall pass?), I came across a small office with another bored-looking guy watching a monitor of the show being taped somewhere else in the building. He was an interesting-looking guy because most of his skin had been burned off, and now he looked a bit like he'd been wrapped in flesh-colored plastic wrap. I said hello and sat down and we watched the daytime talk show host interview one of the guests, a woman who'd been attacked by her boyfriend's dogs and had part of her legs eaten off by them and had to lie in her apartment for two days before anyone found her; luckily, she remembered how to make the tourniquets from her high school first aid class. This guy and I rolled our eyes; not because she'd been partially eaten by dogs, or knew how to make a tourniquet, but because the camera pulled in for a close-up of her face as she cried, and we both understood how sick this whole thing was. All of it. 'We're in the belly of the devil,' my new friend told me. I agreed. It turns out he was a 'back-up' guest, someone who would go on the show only if they ran out of enough horrendous suffering to fill airtime.

Running out of things to fill airtime is the nightmare of all talk show producers. I had a great time once watching producers on a set practically slit their throats as they realized, on a live morning show, that Prince Albert of Monaco, to whom they'd given something like six minutes, which is a *huge* amount of airtime on a morning show (they think it's a big deal to give you two minutes) had absolutely nothing interesting to say. Some now-demoted, inexperienced producer must have figured, Hey, Royalty, he must have six minutes of things to say. Wrong. Of course, *I* had six minutes of things to say, and I would have gladly relieved old Albert out there, added some of his minutes on to my minutes, but I was so enjoying the spectacle of the producers behind the set making wild gestures to one another, to the cameramen and to the gods above that I didn't think of this until it was too late.

I'm always thinking of things too late, especially things I *should* have said. The French have a phrase for it: *esprit d'escalier*. The spirit of the staircase. When you're already leaving, when you're the emotional nude descending the staircase, that's when you think of the exact rejoinder, the perfect thing you *should* have said. It's a bitter journey down that staircase, full of regret; yet another missed opportunity to show someone else just how smart we are, or desirable, or hilarious, how sanguine and wise. It's even worse, let me tell you, when you have a little *esprit d'escalier* on national television. It just so happens I have a whole lot of things I *should* have said to Oprah; at one point I even wanted to call this essay that: 'What I Should Have Said to Oprah'. But then I chickened out. And, to be honest, what I wanted to say to her kept changing. It just so happened that the show I was on for Oprah (this was, alas, before Oprah had started her hit-the-publishing-jackpot book club) was also about people who'd gone through horrendous suffering and become better people for it. It was me, a woman who'd been in a boat wreck and spent days adrift at sea (I liked her; she was a lot of fun), a woman with some kind of disability though I never quite figured out what exactly, and a woman who'd been beaten and treated horrendously as a child. We'd all written books and Oprah openly admitted she'd read none of them, though I was a bit peeved because she kept telling the woman with the horrible childhood what a great writer she was. We each told our stories and then an 'expert' (who'd written his own book about *other* people's suffering, a, get this, 'self-help' book) got to give expert advice about how to deal with horrendous suffering. And, because of the whole empty airtime paranoia, the producers had filled the audience with people with their own horrendous suffering stories, and during the question-and-answer period a woman whose daughter had just been shot or stabbed something like sixty-one times wanted to know what to do. The 'expert' suggested she look 'deep down within herself' for her 'own place of strength'. This prompted me to try to say what I did get to say on the show, in a very bumbled way that I'm sure I'd shoot myself over if I ever watched it (have I mentioned my policy of never actually watching myself on TV? It's the only thing that makes any of this possible), and was something about how truisms only make it more painful for people because simple truisms regarding something as complex as suffering could only make a desperate person feel that much more isolated simply because the truism, which they are being told will help them, which they are being told is the answer, must by definition fail them, and having the *answer* fail you when you've already been beaten to a pulp by the *question* is actually pretty cruel. Or I said something like that; it's all kind of a blur now, and as you can imagine I've spent a fair amount of time revising how I should have worded it so that the blazing truth of it would have changed the face of empathy in America.

But this was only the first *esprit* I suffered through. After I'd had time to think about it, what I wanted to say to Oprah went along the lines of, Hey, why are we four *women*, all of whom have been through actual horrendous suffering, having to sit centered around this *guy* (and he was sitting there, like the king, in the center) just because he's an *expert*, which he is only because he wrote a *self-help* book; I mean, if *we're* not experts and he *is*, then this is a very sorry state of affairs. Or, of course, I could have pointed out to Oprah how her show is built on a series of binarisms that work to differentiate her presented subjectivity, that the show is an attempt to recast the social world and the categorization of groupings in the social world in terms of slightly different definitions and distinctions, and that Oprah is herself a construction of a discourse of the Other. In retrospect of my retrospect, however, I'm sort of glad I *didn't* say that. Or *should* I have said that?

Eventually, my producer came looking for me and found me with my new pal down the hall. Time to go get miked. The second-to-last guest was just starting his tale as she led me down the hall (she was young, perky, skinny, and blond, by the way; I'd heard her right) to the studio, which was in a big ex-ballroom. The actual set was on the other side of a large half wall of some kind of paneling, you could hear the host and guest talking on the other side and see the bright studio lights set up high. I was sat down on a couch on the other side of the paneling; lots of equipment and cables and extra furniture were also sitting around, and there was a monitor that showed what was being taped on the other side of the paneling. The sound was off and everyone on my side of the paneling was very quiet and efficient-looking, holding clipboards and wearing headsets.

The guest was telling his story of being shot in the head and left for dead, and now they were playing a tape of the 911 call that his young boy had made when he found his father lying in the driveway. I can leave, I told myself. I don't have to do this. I don't have to be a part of this, I don't have to acquiesce to the commodification of suffering, to the twisted entertainment we make of it. The producers (there were bunches of them) obviously thought the playing of the

911 tape a brilliant move, and they came around to stand with their clipboards and watch the monitor with me. It seems the guest wasn't expecting to hear the 911 tape, and as the hysterical notes of his young son's voice folded out into the overlit air, he began to sob. The camera pulled in close at first, but then out again so we could see the host bending down on one knee beside him, and then the camera pulled in again so we could see the host's hand moving up to wipe the tears off the man's face. I can leave, I told myself again. But the *realness* of the man's emotions, wrapped up in this, in the most artificial place I'd ever entered, took the power of speech from me. If this was a poem and not an essay, it would end here, the overpowering empty white space of a page the only reasonable answer to what was going on in there. But then my producer put her hand on her heart and said quietly to the others, This is one of the best shows he's ever done, and I came to, to the full force of it *all*, and I wanted to leave again. But then the microphone guy came to me and had to pull me aside and mess around with my sound levels, and then somehow *my* guest was on, and my producer made me go stand on some tape on the floor, in the wings next to the stage but hidden from it. I could hear the host talking to my guest, who was telling his story, but I couldn't really hear it because that 911 tape was still buzzing in my ears, and I could see the audience from where I stood, a busload of mostly nonwhite women who were either clearly bored or intensely moved, one or the other, no in-betweens, and they fascinated me, this audience, because I understood that I *was* them, even though I was also about to be the one they watched. There was a camera on me, and every once in a while its little red light went on, so that I knew I was on TV right then, the sneak preview of the surprise guest.

The first time I thought about what it would be like to be on TV was when I was about seven and saw some footage of the

Beatles at Shea Stadium. So many people watching them, seeing them, loving them. What would it be like, to be *seen* by that many people? Though I couldn't articulate it this way at the time, what I felt was that to be seen by that many people would somehow make you realer than other people. As if your being would shift, like dots in a newsprint photograph, into place, with each dot created by someone else's seeing of you. The more dots, the more in focus you'd become. What was it like, to feel that *real?*

It's easy to poke fun at the stupidity of celebrity, the shallowness of it, just as it's easy to be righteously horrified by the twisted mess the visual media has made of the last century. But what if there's something else at work here? For centuries various scientists have been trying to figure out how flocks of birds and schools of fish are able to move in perfect unison. The assumption's always been that there's one leader, or maybe several leaders, that give the signal to turn, and our attempts to understand the process were simply to seek that leader. Perhaps, we thought, what was stumping us in understanding their turning was that maybe it was some kind of signal we weren't used to, something to do with the earth's magnetic field, or the ability to sense air or water pressure, or to see in a different band of color. Whatever it was, we were looking for it, for that cause, that sign, so that we could understand how and why the others followed it. But this has changed in the last decade or so; now researchers understand more clearly that a flock is its own organism, that a school is not just simply a group of individuals, but that the school itself is an entity, a whole new way of being that is neither individual nor communal, but species based. A whole species is very possibly its own being.

What if a species is to an individual what our sense of self is to our own cells? What if the desire to be famous, to be seen, is some vestigial memory of this, something we lost or forgot about a long time ago? What if being seen by the Others could call that other way of being back? Would we still all feel so alone if this happened? What would it be like, *to be*, to be *seen?*

Finally, the host told my guest they had a little surprise for him. The music came up and I was cued and out I walked, on to the set. My guest's jaw literally dropped. I walked up and the audience clapped and my guest grasped my hand and said, 'I can't believe I'm talking to you.' I smiled and shook his hand and started speaking nervously, saying I don't know what and never will because later my friends told me they cut the sound and all you could hear was the music. Good thing, because I was blathering, I'm sure, trying to hide the fact from several million people that I had just met my stalker face-to-face on a daytime talk show. I heard that voice and knew: You're the person I've never actually seen before, though you did send me pictures which I threw out, who's been calling me relentlessly for the past year, has been sending me letter after letter, strange little gifts I have to put in the garbage because they're so disturbing, you're the person who followed me to a different state, who forced me to get an unlisted phone number, made me give my mail to a friend because I couldn't bear to open it. It made such sense now; who else but a stalker would talk so obsessively about me to a TV producer? If you can't *be* seen, then maybe the next best thing is to *see*, see as loyally, dedicatedly, and intensely as possible. What would it be like, to see someone like that? If you saw them well enough, would that make them *real*? And even if we did see someone as they really are, how would we know it? As soon as the segment ended, I bolted. Maybe I'm delusional, but I never actually felt in danger from my guest, at any point before, during, or since that show. Since the show, in fact, I haven't heard from him even once; maybe finally seeing me in person, shaking my hand, was enough. Maybe, once he saw the real me, the fantasy of me finally stopped haunting him, or bothering him, or teasing him, or whatever it was that the version of me that he saw did to him. The redeeming ridiculous quality here, of course, is that my producer had such a perfect classic daytime talk show topic right there on her own show, and never even knew it.

NERVE

I STARTED OUT MY seductions incognito, as a boy. With my hair shorter than my brothers' had ever been and my thin body almost breastless, the only thing that might have given away my true sex were my rather curvy (though at the time I would only describe them as 'too big') hips. This problem was solved by wearing huge shirts and baggy pants, clothes usually bought in the boys' or men's department of the local thrift store. At one point, at the age of twenty or twenty-one, I was denied entrance to a PG-13-rated movie, the ticket seller under the impression that I was a twelve-year-old boy. A degree of pride deepened my voice when I told my friends about the incident.

A few other times men approached me in the bars I was haunting with my friends. I could see them eyeing me from across the room, and I'd watch them slowly but surely work their way through the crowd toward me.

'What are you drinking?' 'I haven't seen you here before?' 'You look just like someone I know. What's your name?' The lines were ancient and predictable. And just as predictable was the gallant quickness with which these men would scramble away as soon as they heard my high, undeniably female voice reply. This was, after all, a homosexual bar.

I told my friends about these comic scenes too, but I left out crucial elements to the story. I left out how secretly thrilling it was to have these men desire me, even if for only a minute, even if only by mistake. I left out how safe I felt, knowing that I could 'pretend' to be attractive, yet without challenging my deeply ingrained habits of fear. I was afraid, no, make that sure, that I was ugly, that no one would ever want me, that I would die an unloved virgin.

Being 'ugly' was the cause of all my life's despair, of this I was also sure. It was true I had many friends who loved me, but the fact that I didn't have a lover, even by the time I graduated from college, was proof that I would never be a card-carrying member of the sexual world. Beauty was the key to all happiness, and the only way I would ever find love; without it, I was meaningless.

Sex became a litmus test; if, and only if, I could get someone to have sex with me, that would prove I was lovable. I overlooked the fact that all the men I knew were gay, and that I made no attempt whatsoever to find a lover. No, my virginity, my unhappiness, my sense of self, and my face all grew so intertwined that I became unable to respond 'I'm depressed,' when someone asked me how I felt; all I could say, believing this said it all, was, 'I'm ugly.'

During my first year of teaching, I asked my English composition students to write a paper about a time when they were truly afraid. To my surprise, every single one of them wrote about either a ride on a roller coaster, or a horror film they had seen. It's not that I believed they'd had no real fear in their lives, but it struck me as sad and foreboding that they could recognize it clearly only when it happened vicariously. No fear that was directly pointed at them was acknowledgeable. And so it was with me and gay men. Gay men, especially the kind that frequent particular clubs in lower Manhattan, structure their whole personalities around the grammar of sex. My friends throbbed and sweated and grinded around me, spoke constantly in overt innuendos, yet there I was, poor little old me, pretending, while I was secretly learning about sex by osmosis, that none of this had absolutely anything to do with me.

Even at the age of twenty-one, sex was still a murky thing: I wasn't entirely sure how people could bear to look at each other afterward. All those legions of friends who adored me and who told me I was beautiful and lovable meant nothing in the face of such an event; only actual intercourse would convince me I was worth anything at all.

Only a week after my arrival in Iowa, far away from the safely asexual and male homosexual world of college, I lost my virginity. Looking back, I have no doubt I was an easy mark for Jude, the man who had the honors. He was tall and broadly built and extremely chivalrous. We met when I asked him the time at a local auction, where I was buying furniture for my barren apartment. I must have glowed with naïveté, and I know now that this was precisely what attracted him to me, for Jude was without doubt an opportunist and, on many levels, a bastard. He was seventeen years older than I was and deep in the throes of a rather clichéd midlife crisis, which demanded he drive imported sports cars and seduce young virgins. Of course, I did not see it this way at the time.

In my mind, Jude was the most dashing thing going, and I could not believe someone as worldly and as handsome as he would want me. Jude was obsessed with sex. On the good side, he was experienced and taught me both the basics and the exotics: exactly where on a man's penis was the most sensitive; how, while sitting on top of a man, I could vary the speed and depth of the thrusts; that if I hummed as gutturally as possible while performing oral sex it had a quite noticeable effect. He taught me all this openly, even academically, standing or lying there stark naked in his living room, speaking as evenly as if he were teaching me how to use a stick shift. 'You'll drive men wild for the rest of you life,' he told me. The thought filled me with power, yes, but also hope: Someone might one day love me. Somehow, I missed the notion that power had nothing to do with love.

On the bad side, I began to assume some of his philosophies about sex. If maybe I'd been a little too Cinderella-like before, thinking sex was equal to love, now I was slowly becoming exactly the kind of person I'd never quite understood before: someone who could use sex as a weapon, someone who could have sex with someone and have that sex *distance* me from that person. This hit me one day while listening to a Leonard Cohen song in the car, a song about a man leaving a woman. My whole life, up until that point, I'd always identified with the lovelorn woman; suddenly, I realized I identified with the man who just wanted to be free.

It was not just all for his own immediate sexual pleasure that Jude taught me things. Jude, who had been raised in an orphanage, was deeply unable to commit to any one woman, yet, at the same time, was desperate to mean something special to women. Jude wanted me to go out and sleep with other men, but he wanted me always to think of him when I did so. A dedicated emotional manipulator of women himself, he told me how to manipulate men sexually. He taught me how to choose and then perform a specific yet nonsexual act during sex, such as a certain way of stroking a man's forearm, or tapping his elbow. Do this often enough and the act becomes sexualized, so that, in public (and it was important that it be in public), all I had to do was tap my man's elbow and immediately he would get a hard-on. This kind of power astounded me; astounded me that it was *me* who had it, and it astounded me that anyone could be that easily manipulated. Once more, I felt unloved, no longer because a person *wouldn't* have sex with me, but because I now could artfully steer them, trick them, into wanting to have sex with me.

Jude also taught me about the complicated relationship most men have to their anuses, how sexually charged yet humiliating this charge is for them, how, if I could break that barrier with them subtly and correctly, they would become dependent upon me to provide that secret pleasure for them. And so a new level was yet again introduced: Now I could not only convince men to have sex with me, and then resent them for it, but I could, if I used their own desires against them, cause them to resent *me* for it. Jude's world was all about emotional dominance and manipulation, about tricking people into becoming obsessed with you, and, ultimately, about the total absence of love. I had come full circle.

But I'm getting ahead of myself here. In one year I went from dressing like a boy to becoming a seductress: quite a swing of the pendulum. Once Jude had me under his sexual wing, he started instructing me in how to dress. Short leather skirts, high heels, garter belts. These were items I'd never have considered wearing only a short time before, but the simple fact that Jude was 'willing' to sleep with me gave him power over me. And even though I still hated my face, I had to admit I had a good body. Yet the scant clothing I wore became just as much a costume as my asexual garb had been previously: It hid me from myself, from my own fears. I became dependent upon the clothes to the point where I could not even go to the grocery store without dressing up.

Before I'd ever had sex, I saw it only as a way to prove that I was not ugly, and therefore lovable. Yet because of the flaw in that equation, that sex equaled love, I remained feeling ugly and unloved even after I became sexually active. And because it is a hidden flaw, hidden by Hollywood and television and cultural history in general, I truly believed my persistent feelings of ugliness meant that I was not having *enough* sex, or *good enough* sex. This was, after all, easier than the more difficult option of having to reconsider the basic truth of the equation itself. Despite the fact that all I really wanted was for one special person to love me, I persisted in believing I could only conjure this person by being as sexual with as many people as possible.

At Jude's urging, and even long after we had our final split, I went out and seduced men whenever and wherever I could. A lyric from another Leonard Cohen song, a song I'd previously not 'gotten', became something of a motto: Life is filled with many sweet companions, many satisfying one-night stands. Almost any kind of behavior can work if you have the right motto (though I completely resisted the definition that I was 'acting out'.) Vaguely, I reasoned that each man I slept with brought me five to six inches closer to the man who would ultimately love me. Bent on proving I was desirable, I worked my way through a series of affairs that always ended, I was absolutely certain, because I wasn't beautiful enough. Convinced that anyone who might actually want to have a relationship with me was someone I didn't want, I invariably began hurting people, though of course I never saw this. If they regretted my leaving (my favorite ploy was simply to move to another city or even another country), I simply did not believe I could matter that much. I felt I had only tricked them into loving me, and therefore their love could never be genuine. In retrospect, I see my lovers dropped me many hints, but at the time I thought it was all about *more*.

There was no easy way to climb out of this cycle, which cavorted on for years. Each man offered some type of power: I slept with a friend's boyfriend because it made me feel sexier than her, I slept with a plastic surgeon (not my own) in his examining room because it made me feel less like a patient, and I slept with numerous married men because, perversely, I wanted to be married. I slept with sleazeballs because I thought it would prove I didn't care, I slept with drunks because I was drunk, and I slept with men I hated because I thought it would prove I would do anything for love.

Though often sorrowful throughout the years of my sexual rabidness, I do not want this to stand as a parable on the virtues of monogamy. What caused my sadness and my deep-seated insatiability was not any moral breakdown on my part, a moral breakdown any number of conservative cultural watchdogs would love to claim is proved by the sheer numbers of my lovers, but rather I was lonely and oversexed because I had fallen for the old lie that beauty equals worthiness. All that sex, a lot of which I actually enjoyed, was an attempt to prove that I could be loved. The issue of sex itself, so often used as a symbol of decadence, was innocent. My own unwillingness, or inability, to recognize all the subtle clues that beauty is only an easy label for a complex set of emotions (feelings of safety and grace and well-being) were what hurt me in the end. It was easy to ascribe to physical beauty these qualities that I thought I could earn through sex; there were not many clues around me to the contrary. And when sex did not deliver that sense of well-being I was looking for, it remained easier yet to think I still wasn't beautiful or sexy enough than to confront the complex possibility that perhaps these qualities did not really belong to this thing I called beauty after all.

Most important to my blindness, I think, was my belief that I was in this alone, that it was only me who ever had any doubts about any of this. Though very subtly, without my ever knowing it consciously, my sexual and emotional life were slowly forming some kind of underground harmony. Consciously, however, I still did not recognize sex as a shared experience: I saw it as a contest, two people in different rooms trying to push various buttons, despite all the hints that Fate itself was dropping me. I remember, once, having sex inside a wax museum in Berlin with one of the curators. He was a very handsome curator, a bit like Paul Newman, but with bad teeth. We were behind the Franz Liszt display, where a dusty Liszt in a yellow brocaded coat mechanically and repeatedly bent over and then sat up in front of a piano that was playing the same solo over and over again. My lover and I fruitlessly rubbed against each other. Museum patrons kept clopping past us, hidden from view by a fake wall.

'I think this I can't do,' he finally told me in his heavy accent, sitting up. 'Too many people. And I keep thinking how I could lose my job.'

'But you do think I'm attractive, don't you?' I asked him, worried again.

He looked at me quizzically for a long moment, the piano starting again at the beginning of its loop. 'Of course,' he said, and paused again, a line of deep and serious concern on his face. 'We both are. It is the music that makes us so.'

MIRRORINGS

THERE WAS A LONG period of time, almost a year, during which I never looked in a mirror. It wasn't easy, for I'd never suspected just how omnipresent are our own images. I began by merely avoiding mirrors, but by the end of the year I found myself with an acute knowledge of the reflected image, its numerous tricks and wiles, how it can spring up at any moment: a glass tabletop, a well-polished door handle, a darkened window, a pair of sunglasses, a restaurant's otherwise magnificent brass-plated coffee machine sitting innocently by the cash register.

At the time, I had just moved, alone, to Scotland and was surviving on the dole, Britain's social security benefits. I didn't know anyone and had no idea how I was going to live, yet I went anyway because by happenstance I'd met a plastic surgeon there who said he could help me. I'd been living in London, working temp jobs. While in London, in only the first three weeks, I'd received more nasty comments about my face than I had in the previous three years, living in Iowa, New York, and Germany. These comments, all from men and all odiously sexual, hurt and disoriented me. I also had journeyed to Scotland because after more than a dozen operations in the States my insurance had run out, along with my hope that further operations could make any *real* difference. Here, however, was a surgeon who had some new techniques, and here, amazingly enough, was a government willing to foot the bill. I didn't feel I could pass up yet another chance to 'fix' my face, which I confused with 'fixing' my self, my soul, my life.

Twenty years earlier, when I was nine and living in America, I came home from school one day with a toothache. Several weeks and misdiagnoses later, surgeons removed most of the right side of my jaw in an attempt to prevent the cancer they found there from spreading. No one properly explained the operations to me, and I awoke in a cocoon of pain that prevented me from moving or speaking. Tubes ran in and out of my body, and because I was temporarily unable to speak after the surgery and could not ask questions, I made up my own explanations for the tubes' existence. I remember the mysterious manner the adults displayed toward me. They asked me to do things: lie still for X-rays, not cry for needles, and so on, tasks that, although not easy, never seemed equal to the praise I received in return. Reinforced to me again and again was how I was a 'brave girl' for not crying, a 'good girl' for not complaining, and soon I began defining myself this way, equating strength with silence.

Then the chemotherapy began. In the 1970's chemo was even cruder than it is now, the basic premise being to poison patients right up to the brink of their own death. Until this point I almost never cried and almost always received praise in return. Thus I got what I considered the better part of the deal. But now, it was like a practical joke that had gotten out of hand. Chemotherapy was a nightmare and I wanted it to stop; I didn't want to be brave anymore. Yet I had grown so used to defining myself as 'brave' – i.e., silent – that the thought of losing this definition of myself was even more terrifying. I was certain that if I broke down I would be despicable in the eyes of both my parents and the doctors.

The task of taking me into the city for the chemo injections fell mostly on my mother, though sometimes my father made the trip. Overwhelmed by the sight of the vomiting and weeping, my father developed the routine of 'going to get the car', meaning that he left the doctor's office before the injection was administered, on the premise that then he could have the car ready and waiting when it was all over. Ashamed of my suffering – I felt it was a personal failure, that I suffered, that I could not hide my suffering – I watched his back as he left and felt relief, because his embarrassment and awkwardness caused me as much pain as they did him. There was no blame in those moments, no regrets, no accusations, not even despair. Those things came later, when I learned to scrutinize and judge the past, but at the time his leaving was enabling. Knowing that my father had his own burdens, his own failings, allowed me to continue on through what would otherwise have been unbearable. As an adult, I wonder how he could have left me alone in there, but as a child I knew the answer to this clearly, and knew that as soon as he was out of the room I was, if nothing else, free to respond as *I* chose. My father's nervous whistling of Bobby Sherman's *Julie, Julie, do you love me* faded down the hall as the doctor turned to me with his tourniquet and I turned to him with my unfettered grief.

It was different with my mother. Raised during the war, in England, it was she who taught me that the best way to deal with fear was not to show it, that any display, even the smallest crack, would invite an overwhelming flood of the stuff; best to remain staunch and, in this particular situation, not cry. Each week she urged me not to cry and each week I tried my best and always, as I saw it, failed. My sense of failure only added new layers to my suffering, which only gave me that much more to hide, and on and on it went, week after week for two and a half years.

Once in a while, however, because suffering is a teacher, I experienced moments of transcendence there on the chemotherapy table, moments in which I felt compassion for my mother's taut face, for my own small self, even for the doctor, his cold-fish exterior suddenly exposed to me as the painfully applied veneer of a damaged man. But they were only moments, and in the next moment, when I found myself suffering again, I felt that I had failed in some spiritual way simply because I could not make those moments of comfort stay, nor could I, at will, summon them back.

In the midst of all this pain, though, there were other moments of relief. Each week, two or three days after the injection, there came the first flicker of feeling better, the always forgotten and gratefully rediscovered understanding that simply to be well in my body was the greatest thing I could ask for. I thought other people felt this appreciation and physical joy all the time, and I felt cheated because I was able to feel it only once a week.

Because I'd lost my hair, I wore a hat constantly, but this fooled no one, least of all myself. During this time, my mother worked in a nursing home in a Hasidic community. Hasidic law dictates that married woman cover their hair, and most women did this with a wig. My mother's friends were all too willing to donate their discarded wigs, and soon the house was filled with them. I never wore one, for they frightened me even when my mother insisted I looked better in one of the few that actually fit. Yet we didn't know how to say no to the women who kept graciously offering their wigs. The cats slept on them and the dogs played with them, and we grew used to having to pick a wig up off a chair in order to sit down. It never struck us as odd until one day a visitor commented wryly as he cleared a chair for himself, and suddenly a wave of shame overcame me. I had nightmares about wigs and flushed if I even heard the word, and one night I put myself out of my misery by getting up after everyone was asleep and gathering all the wigs except for one the dogs were fond of and that they had chewed up anyway. I hid all the rest in an old trunk.

When you are only ten, which is when the chemotherapy began, two and a half years seem like your whole life, yet it did finally end, for the cancer was gone. I remember the last day of treatment clearly because it was the only day on which I succeeded in not crying and because afterward, in private, I cried harder than I had in years because I thought now I would no longer be 'special', that without the arena of chemotherapy in which to prove myself no one would ever love me, know I was worthy of love, and that I would fade unnoticed into the background. But this idea about not being different didn't last very long. Before, I had foolishly believed that people stared at me because I was bald. After my hair grew in, it didn't take long before I understood that I looked different for another reason. My face. People stared at me in stores, and other children made fun of me to the point that I came to expect such reactions constantly, wherever I went. School became a battleground.

Halloween became my favorite holiday because I could put on a mask and walk among the blessed for a few brief, sweet hours. Such freedom I felt, walking down the street, my face hidden. Through the imperfect oval holes I could peer out at other faces, masked or painted or not, and see on those faces nothing but the normal faces of childhood looking back at me, faces I mistakenly thought were the faces everyone else but me saw all the time, not the faces I usually braced myself for, the cruel, lonely, vicious ones I spent every day other than Halloween waiting to see around each corner. As I breathed in the condensed, plastic-scented air beneath the mask, I thought I was breathing in normalcy, that this joy and weightlessness were what the world was composed of, and that it was only my face that kept me from it, my face that was my own mask that kept me from knowing the joy I felt sure everyone but me lived with intimately. How could the others not know it? Not know that to be free of the fear of taunts and the burden of knowing no one would ever love you was all that anyone could ever ask for? I was a pauper walking for a few brief hours in the clothes of the prince, and when the day ended and I gave up my disguise, I felt both sad and relieved. Sad because I had liked feeling those feelings and didn't want them to end. Relieved because I felt no connection to that kind of happiness: I didn't deserve it and thus I shouldn't want it. It was easier to blame my face for everything.

I was living in an extreme situation, and because I did not particularly care for the world I was in, I lived in others, and because the world I did live in was dangerous now, I incorporated this danger into my secret life. I imagined myself to be an Indian. Walking down the streets, I stepped through the forest, my body ready for any opportunity to fight or flee one of the big cats I knew stalked me. Vietnam and Cambodia, in the news then as scenes of catastrophic horror, were other places I walked through daily. I made my way down the school hall knowing a land mine or sniper might give themselves away at any moment with the subtle metal click I'd read about. Compared with a land mine, a mere insult about my face seemed a frivolous thing.

In those years, not yet a teenager, I read works by Primo Levi and Elie Wiesel and every other book by a survivor I could find. Auschwitz, Birkenau: I felt the blows of the capos and somehow knew that because at any moment we might be called upon to live for a week on one loaf of bread and some water called soup, the peanut-butter sandwich I found on my plate was nothing less than a miracle, an utter and sheer miracle capable of making me literally weep with joy.

I decided to become a 'deep' person. I wasn't exactly sure what this would entail, but I believed that if I could just find the right philosophy, think the right thoughts, my suffering would end. To try to understand the world I was in, I undertook to find out what was 'real', and I quickly began seeing reality as existing in the lowest common denominator, that suffering was the one and only dependable thing. But rather than spend all of my time despairing, though I certainly did plenty of that, I developed a form of defensive egomania: I felt I was the only one walking about in the world who understood what was really important. I looked upon people complaining about the most mundane things – nothing on TV, traffic jams, the price of new clothes – and felt joy because I knew how unimportant those things really were, and felt unenlightened superiority because other people didn't. Because in my fantasy life I had learned to be thankful for each cold, blanketless night that I survived on the cramped wooden bunks, my pain and despair were a stroll through the country in comparison. I was often miserable, but I knew that to feel warm instead of cold was its own kind of joy, that to eat was a reenactment of the grace of some god whom I could only dimly define, and that simply to be alive was a rare, ephemeral gift.

As I became a teenager, my isolation began. My nonidentical twin sister started going out with boys, and I started – my most tragic mistake of all – to listen to and believe the taunts thrown at me daily by the very boys she and the other girls were interested in. I was a dog, a monster, the ugliest girl they had ever seen. Of all the remarks, the most damaging wasn't even directed at me but was really an insult to Jerry, a boy I never saw because every day between fourth and fifth periods, when I was cornered by this particular group of kids, I was too ashamed to lift my eyes off the floor. 'Hey, look, it's Jerry's girlfriend!' they shrieked when they saw me, and I felt such shame, knowing that this was the deepest insult to Jerry that they could imagine.

When pressed to it, one makes compensations. I came to love winter, when I could wrap up the disfigured lower half of my face in a scarf; I could speak to people and they would have no idea to whom and what they were really speaking. I developed the bad habits of letting my long hair hang in my face and of always covering my chin and mouth with my hand, hoping it might be mistaken as a thoughtful, accidental gesture. I also became interested in horses and got a job at a run-down local stable. Having those horses to go to each day after school saved my life; I spent all of my time either with them or thinking about them. Completely and utterly repressed by the time I was sixteen, I was convinced that I would never want a boyfriend, not ever, and wasn't it convenient for me, even a blessing, that no one would ever want me. I told myself I was free to concentrate on the 'true reality' of life, something which had nothing to do with the ephemeral world of boys, of that much I was sure. My sister and her friends put on blue eye shadow, blow-dried their hair, and spent interminable hours at the local mall, and I looked down on them for this, knew they were misleading themselves and being overly occupied with the 'mere surface' of living. I'd thought like this when I was younger, ten or twelve, but now my philosophy was haunted by desires so frightening I was unable even to admit they existed.

Throughout all of this, I was undergoing reconstructive surgery in an attempt to rebuild my jaw. It started when I was fifteen, two years after the chemo ended. I had known for years I would have operations to 'fix' my face, and at night I fantasized about how good my life would finally be then. One day I got a clue that maybe it wouldn't be so easy. An older plastic surgeon explained the process by which he would create 'tubes' of skin on my stomach and then 'harvest' those tubes of skin and sew them on to my face. Also, he said rather nonchalantly, it would take ten years. Ten years? Why even bother? I thought; I'll be ancient by then. I went to a medical library and looked up the procedure he talked about. In these books I found gruesome pictures of people with grotesque flaps of skin hanging off them, pictures of people who, to my mind, looked just as bad in the 'after' pictures as they did in the 'before'. But then I met a younger surgeon, who was working on a new way of grafting that involved giving the graft its own blood supply, and I became more hopeful and once again began to await the fixing of my face, the day when I would be whole, content, loved.

Long-term reconstructive plastic surgery is not like it is in the movies. There is no one single operation that will change everything, and there is certainly no slow unwrapping of the gauze in order to view the final, remarkable result. There is always swelling, often grotesque swelling, there are bruises, there are always scars. After each operation, too frightened to go simply look in the mirror, I developed an oblique method, with several stages. First, I tried to catch my reflection in an overhead lamp: the roundness of the metal distorted my image just enough to obscure details and give no true sense of size or proportion. Then I slowly worked my way up to looking at the reflection in someone's eyeglasses, and from there I went to walking by a mirror, glancing only quickly. I repeated this as many times as it would take me, passing the mirror slightly more slowly each time until finally I was able to stand still and confront myself.

The theory behind most reconstructive surgery is to take large chunks of muscle, skin, and bone and slap them into the roughly appropriate place, then slowly begin to carve this mess into some sort of shape. It involves long, major operations, countless lesser ones, a lot of pain, and many, many years. And also, it does not always work. With my young surgeon in New York, who with each passing year was becoming not so young, I had two or three soft-tissue grafts, two skin grafts, a bone graft, an some dozen other operations to 'revise' my face, yet when I left graduate school at the age of twenty-five I was still more or less in the same position I had started in: a deep hole in the right side of my face and a rapidly shrinking left side and chin, a result, among other things, of the radiation I'd had as a child. I was caught in a cycle of having a big operation, one that would force me to look monstrous from the swelling for many months, then having the subsequent revision operations that improved my looks, and then slowly, over the period of a few months or a year, watching the graft reabsorb back into my body, slowly shrinking down and leaving me with nothing but the scarred donor site the graft had originally come from.

It wasn't until I was in college that I finally allowed that maybe, just maybe, it might be nice to have a boyfriend. I went to a small, liberal, predominantly female school and suddenly, after years of loneliness in high school, discovered that there were other people I could enjoy talking to who thought me intelligent and talented. I was, however, still operating on the assumption that no one, not ever, would be physically attracted to me, and in a curious way this shaped my personality. I became forthright and honest in the way that only the truly self-confident are, those who don't expect to be rejected, and in the way of those like me, who do not even dare to ask acceptance from others and therefore also expect no rejection. I had come to know myself as a person, but I would be in graduate school before I was literally, physically able to use my name and the word *woman* in the same sentence.

Now my friends repeated for me endlessly that most of it

was in mind, that, granted, I did not look like everyone else, but that didn't categorically mean I looked bad. I'm sure they were right some of the time. But with the constant surgery I was in a perpetual state of transfiguration. I rarely looked the same for more than six months at a time. So ashamed of my face, I was unable even to admit this constant change affected me; I let everyone who wanted to know that it was only what was inside that mattered, that I had 'grown used to' the surgery, that none of it bothered me at all. Just as I had done in childhood, I pretended nothing was wrong, and this was constantly mistaken by others for bravery. I spent a great deal of time looking in the mirror in private, positioning my head to show my eyes and nose, which were not only normal but quite pretty, as my friends told me often. But I could not bring myself to see them for more than a moment: I looked in the mirror and saw only the reasons why I would be alone for the rest of my life.

People still teased me. Not daily, as when I was younger, but in ways that caused me more pain than ever before. Children stared at me, and I learned to cross the street to avoid them; this bothered me, but not as much as the insults I got from men. Their taunts came at me not because I was disfigured but because I was a disfigured *woman*. They came from boys, sometimes from men, and almost always from a group of them. I had long, blond hair and a thin figure. Sometimes, from a distance, men would see the thin blonde and whistle, something I dreaded more than anything else because I knew that as they got closer, their tune, so to speak, would change; they'd stare openly or, worse, turn away quickly. I decided to cut my hair to avoid any misconception that anyone, however briefly, might have about my being attractive. Only two or three times have I ever been teased by a single person, and I can think of only one time when I was ever teased, openly, by a woman. Had I been a man, would I have had to walk down the street while a group of young women followed and denigrated my sexual worth?

Not surprisingly, then, I viewed sex as my salvation. I was sure that if only I could get someone to sleep with me, it would mean I wasn't ugly, that I was attractive, even lovable. This line of reasoning led me into the beds of several men who liked themselves even less than they liked me and I in turn left each short-term affair hating myself, obscenely sure that if only I had been prettier it would have worked – he would have loved me and it would have been like those other love affairs I was certain normal women had all the time.

The new surgeon in Scotland, Oliver Fenton, recommended that I undergo a procedure involving something called a tissue expander, followed by a bone graft. A tissue expander is a small balloon placed under the skin and then slowly blown up over the course of several months, the object being to stretch out the skin and create room and cover for the new bone. It's a bizarre, nightmarish thing to do to your face, yet I was hopeful about the end results and I was also able to spend the three months that the expansion took in the hospital. I've always felt safe in hospitals; they're the one place I felt free from the need to explain the way I look. For this reason the first tissue expander was bearable – just – and the bone graft that followed it was a success; it did not melt away like the previous ones.

The stress all this put upon what remained of my original jaw instigated the deterioration of that bone, however, and it became unhappily apparent that I was going to need the same operation I'd just had on the right side done to the left. I remember my surgeon telling me this at an outpatient clinic. I planned to be traveling to London that same night on an overnight train, and I barely made it to the station on time, such a fumbling state of despair was I in.

I could not imagine going through it *again*, and just as I had done all my life, I searched and searched my intellect for a way to make it OK, make it bearable, for a way to *do* it. I lay awake all night on that train, the tracks slipping beneath my narrow bed with an odd eroticism, and thought of an afternoon from my three months in the hospital. Boredom was a big problem those long afternoons, the days marked by meals and what was on television. Waiting for the afternoon tea to come, wondering desperately how I could make time pass, it had suddenly occurred to me that I didn't have to *make* time pass, that it would do it of its own accord, that I could relax and take no action. Lying on the train, remembering this, I realized I had no obligation to make this OK, that I didn't have to explain or understand it. Sometimes, we can just let our lives *happen*. By the time the train pulled into King's Cross, I felt able to bear it yet again, not entirely sure what other choice I had.

But there was an element I didn't yet know about. When I returned to Scotland to set up a date to have the tissue expander inserted, I was told quite casually that I'd be in the hospital only three or four days. Wasn't I going to spend the whole expansion time in the hospital? I asked in a whisper. What's the point of that? came the answer. You can just come in everyday to the outpatient ward and have it expanded. Horrified by this, I was speechless. I would have to live and move about in the outside world with a balloon inside my cheek? I spent the next few days drinking in bars. The night before I went into the hospital I even allowed a man to pick me up, and while I was with him I kept thinking how he had no idea who and what he was really with.

I had the operation and went home at the end of the week. The only things that gave me any comfort during the months I lived with my face gradually ballooning out were my writing and reading. I wrote for hours each day and lost myself in everything from Kafka to Jackie Collins. I'd usually walk to the hospital, even though it was several miles, because I didn't want to get on the bus and feel trapped that way. Luckily it was also cold, so I could wrap my whole head up in a scarf. As the tissue expander grew and grew, this became harder to do. I stopped going out except to the hospital and the little store around the corner from me to buy food. I'd become familiar with the man who worked there, and I kept wondering when he was going to ask what was wrong. I assumed they thought I had some massive tumor and were afraid to ask.

Finally I couldn't stand the polite silence any longer. I blurted out my whole life story to the man behind the counter. I was holding a glass bottle of milk, letting the whole saga stream out of me, when the bells tied to the door jangled. A man completely, and I mean completely, covered in tattoos walked in. I stopped in midsentence and stared at him. He stopped in midstride and stared at me. There was a puma reaching across his cheek to his nose, which had some kind of tree on it, the trunk of it running along the bridge and then flowering up on his forehead. He hadn't even one inch of naturally colored skin; his ears, neck, and hands were covered with lush jungle scenes and half-naked women with seashells covering their breasts.

We finally broke our mutual stares, I paid for my milk, he bought a pack of cigarettes, and we walked out together, turning different ways at the corner. In the same way that imagining living in Cambodia had helped me as a child, I walked the streets of my dark little Scottish city by the sea and knew without a doubt that I was living in a story Kafka would have been proud to write.

This time period, however, was also the time I stopped looking in the mirror. I simply didn't want to know. Many times before in my life have I been repelled by the mirror, but the repulsion always took the form of a strange, obsessive attraction. Previously I spent many hours looking in the mirror, trying to see what it was that other people were seeing, a purpose I understand now was laughable, as I went to the mirror with an already clearly fixed, negative idea of what people were seeing. Once I even remember quickly passing a mirror in a shopping center, thinking how awful I looked, seeing perfectly all the flaws I knew were there, when I realized with a shock that I wasn't looking in a mirror, that I was looking through a window into a store at someone who had the same coat and haircut as I, someone who, when I examined closer, looked perfectly fine.

The one good thing about a tissue expander is that you look so bad with it in that no matter what you look like once it's finally removed, it *has* to be better. I had my bone graft and my fifth soft-tissue graft and, yes, even I had to admit I looked better. But I didn't look like *me*. Something was wrong: Was *this* the face I had waited through twenty years and almost thirty operations for? I somehow just couldn't make what I saw in the mirror correspond to the person I thought I was. It wasn't just that I felt ugly, I simply could not associate the image as belonging to me. My own image was the image of a stranger, and rather than try to understand this, I simply ignored it. I reverted quickly back to my tissue expander mode of not looking in the mirror, and quickly improved it to include not looking at *any* image of myself. I perfected the technique of brushing my teeth without a mirror, grew my hair in such a way that it would require only a quick simple brush, and wore clothes that were simply and easily put on, no complex layers or lines that might require even the most minor of visual adjustments.

On one level I understood that the image of my face was merely that, an image, a surface which was not directly related to any true, deep definition of the self. But I also knew that it is only through image that we experience and make decisions about the everyday world, and I was not always able to gather the strength to prefer the deeper world over the shallower one. I looked for ways to relate the two, to find a bridge that would allow me access to both, anything no matter how tenuous, rather than ride out the constant swings between peace and anguish. The only direction I had to go in to achieve this was to simply strive for a state of awareness and self-honesty that sometimes, to this day, rewards me, and sometimes exhausts me.

Our whole lives are dominated, though it is not always so clearly translatable, with the question 'How do I look?' Take all the many nouns in our lives – car, house, job, family, love, friends – and substitute the personal pronoun. It is not that we are all so self-obsessed, it is that all things eventually relate back to ourselves, and it is our own sense of how we appear to the world by which we chart our lives, how we navigate our personalities which would otherwise be adrift in the ocean of *other* people's obsessions.

One particular afternoon I remember very lucidly, an afternoon toward the end of my year-long separation from the mirror. I was talking to someone, an attractive man as it happened, and we were having a wonderful, engaging conversation. And perhaps because he was attractive it flickered across my mind to wonder what I looked like to him. What was he seeing when he saw me? So many times I've asked this of myself, and always the answer was a bad one, an ugly one. A warm, smart woman, yes, but still, an unattractive one. I sat there in the café and asked myself this old question and, startlingly, for first time in my life I had no answer readily prepared. I had literally not looked in a mirror for so long that I quite simply had no clue as to what I looked like. I gazed at the man as he spoke; my entire life I had been giving my negative image to people, handing it to them and watching the negative way it was reflected back to me. But now, because I had no idea what I was giving him, the only thing I had to judge by was what he was giving me, which, as reluctant as I was to admit it, was positive.

That afternoon in that café I had a moment of the freedom I had been practicing for behind my Halloween mask as a child. But whereas as a child I expected it to come as a result of gaining something, a new face, it came to me then as the result of shedding something, of shedding my image. I once thought that truth was eternal, that once you understood something it was with you forever, a constant by which you could measure everything else. I know now that this isn't so, that most truths are inherently unretainable, that we have to work hard all our lives to remember the most basic things. Society is no help; the images it gives us again and again want us only to believe that we can most be ourselves by looking like someone else, leaving our own faces behind to turn into ghosts that will inevitably come to resent and haunt us. It is no mistake that in books and films the newly dead sometimes are only completely convinced of their deadness after being offered the most irrefutable proof of all: They can no longer see themselves in the mirror. And as I sat there feeling the warmth of the cup against my palm, this small observation seemed like a great revelation to me, and I wanted to tell the man I was with about it, but he was involved in his own topic and I did not want to interrupt him, so instead I looked with curiosity over to the window behind him, its night-silvered glass reflecting the whole café, to see if I could, now, recognize myself.

WHAT IT TAKES

FOR ONLY TEN DOLLARS, you can get an hour introductory class *and* a half-hour private lesson at most of New York's dancing 'academies'. When I finally decided, at the age of thirty-two, to learn the tango proper, I was surprised and a little pleased by the pages and pages of dance schools listed in the yellow pages. Just by their ads I could tell these businesses were fiercely competitive. I knew the ten dollars was only the wiggling worm, the first free fix, yet I anticipated with a very basic pleasure being fawned over, sold something. In the end, however, all the schools seemed the same, and I chose the school that claimed to have taught a famous actor to dance; it seemed an appropriately random enough reason on which to base a decision.

It was summer, and all of us in the first introductory class were embarrassingly freshly showered and sweaty and smelling of toothpaste. If the rest were anything like me, then each of us had anticipated that fateful encounter with our one true love, whom we'd recognize at a glance across the floor, while simultaneously anticipating a room full of desperate clods, and obviously each of us had figured, in the face of either event, that we should at least be clean. The class ran this way: Anthony, the group instructor, would show us a basic step, then have the men and women form different lines. The lines would collide to form separate couples, then each couple would try out the step as Anthony counted out the timing for us. Next came the order 'Switch!' and each woman would rotate clockwise to the next man. There were fifteen women and eleven men, which meant that there were always four women during each rotation who had a choice: stand still and watch the couples on either side work out their figures, or hold out your arms and practice your steps with a ghost. Early on, I figured this was some sort of character test, and I watched to see who would stand and how awkwardly they would stand, and who would dance and how unselfconsciously they would dance.

When I finally got around to taking tango lessons, which is to say when I finally got over my humiliation of wanting to take tango lessons, it was the small gestures that surprised me; the slight push of my partner's hand, the brush of his knee on my inner thigh, his persistent fingers on my back. It was so intimate, and this intimacy was so public, and ran so parallel to the impersonal, it was pornographic. And every time I thought this, felt the slight stir of sex, and the faint shame of sex, I felt even more ashamed, and even more sexed by the indifferent, formal framework of our meeting.

My private instructor's name is Ivan and he possesses a strong Slavic accent and even stronger Slavic face. Our first few lessons together I want to ask him if tango is popular among Eastern European immigrants, or if he's an exception. I want to ask him all about his life because I love anyone different, but I don't because not only might it be rude, but I also actively remind myself that I'm only one of many students. He's got a strong, well-proportioned face and blue eyes, thick black hair, and skin so white you can see the beard beneath its just-shaven smoothness. I'm sure that with the close physical contact many students develop a crush, and I decide almost immediately that I will absolutely not fall into such a rut. Instead, I decide, he should develop a crush on me. It's an almost arbitrary decision. After all, the school has at least half a dozen male dance instructors, and I could have been paired with any of them. Ivan has come into my life like the majority of my friends and most of my lovers: with an erratic luck.

In truth, I've wanted to tango ever since I first saw Gomez grab Morticia in a TV sitcom from my childhood, *The Addams Family*. The show was based on a series of *New Yorker* cartoons by Charles Addams which focused on the lifestyle of a particularly macabre family. The cartoon characters were ghoulish and droll, and the producers of the TV show spent the first season trying to duplicate this. But it wasn't their oddness that attracted me, for I was odd myself, something I alternately courted and despised. The Addamses, for all their quirkiness, were still a very tight-knit family; the producers quickly picked up on this and later episodes underscored the Addamses 'functional' attributes. Essentially, *The Addams Family* went from being about outsiders to *Father Knows Best* in drag. And while the Addamses retained their genuine eccentricities even with the tinkering of their family dynamics, this was still an era in which the shape of television sitcoms distinctly American were being defined. Unlike earlier comedies, which traced their roots to rowdy and uncensored vaudeville, most sitcoms in this country after World War II consisted of episodes built around recurring, easily digested morals. Typically, these morals underscored honesty and hard work. Oddly, these morals were usually 'learned' by eventually becoming discovered as the actions which would have prevented the preceding half hour of comedic antics in the first place. Whatever immoral fun took place could be presented by producers 'safe' in the knowledge that ultimately it was all for the 'good'.

Still, when I was watching the Addamses, and without

knowing how little I knew, I had only exaggerated, silhouetted impressions of what made a tango a tango. Along with my friends, tango, to our adolescent minds, was like sex or our crippled math teacher, or what we thought sounded very much like Chinese; all things easily made fun of. On a regular basis throughout elementary and junior high school, usually accompanied by fits of insidious laughter, I would find myself grabbing someone's arm in mine, dramatically pointing it straight out toward one end of the room, and then following it with a stealthy, sidling gait, all to be followed some ten steps later by the abrupt maneuver and thrill of dramatically changing arms and direction so as to glide awkwardly, no matter how slick I believed we looked, back to our original starting point.

But unlike mimicking the math teacher and chortling in pseudo-Chinese, tango continued to stake its claim on my desires even in private. And because I didn't know what real tango was, the tango I actually desired was the laden moment itself, when the mood would overcome Gomez – it seemed a mood which easily overtook him, and I wanted that impetuousness as well – and Gomez would yell, 'Tang-go!' abruptly turning his torso and full attention – and, oh, how I wanted attention turned on me with such focus – toward Morticia, tossing whatever he was holding behind him, not caring if it was a priceless vase or ticking bomb (yes, I wanted that too, that knowledge of how worth was fluid, that money and danger were valueless when up against passion), simply so that he, Gomez, could better stretch out his open hand toward his beloved wife. Whatever else was going on, when Gomez and Morticia had to tango, they tangoed.

As I was performing my own pseudo tango in those childhood basements, I had no idea just how complicated the tango was, and complicated not just in its actual maneuvers, but in its very tangled and shadowy history.

My first surprise was to learn just how sad tango is. That very first group lesson, Anthony, the head instructor, emphasized the importance of 'tango face'. 'You have to look like you just came from a funeral,' he told us. You rarely, if ever, look your partner in the eyes, something which distinguishes tango from most other dances.This sadness is embedded in the physical gestures of tango, but is easiest to see in the lyrics of tango songs. Love in tango is not the simple 'boy meets girl and they live happily ever after' type of love. Most tangos are about suffering from love. And if they aren't about suffering from love, then they are about suffering from poverty or social oppression. Their lyrics outline lives filled with bad luck, hunger, isolation and God's indifference. One of the best known definitions of tango comes from Carlos Gardel, one of the great tango singers of all time. 'It's like dancing a sad thought,' he said.

As soon as this unexpected underside of tango showed itself to me, I became even more curious. I set out to learn as much as I could. The basic, physical facts were easy: A defining feature that separates tango from ballroom dances (even though tango is often defined as a ballroom dance, to the horror of its purists) is timing. Except on the contest floor, it's not a neatly laid out dance. It's a lot like jazz, with the lead dancer improvising, slowing down and speeding up as he feels the need, doing whatever figure he fancies at that precise moment. It's tango's lack of choreography, its reliance on inventiveness, which makes a lot of traditional ballroom dancers avoid it; most people tend to favor the more structured, 'safer' dances, such as the waltz and foxtrot.

But it was the history of tango – it took a while for me to get familar enough with it to drop the article 'the' – that surprised me most of all. Its origins are still under debate. In Argentina, tango is widely danced by all levels of society, and is endless fodder for Argentinean intellectuals and a source of cultural identity for nonintellectuals. There, the debate over tango's history gets vicious, with ruined marriages, lost tenure, and even, in at least one case, a duel. There are thirty-three official histories of tango, but most people agree that ur-tango first appeared in the mid-1800's in the Río de la Plata region of South America, the region that has a foot in both Brazil and Uruguay, and then culminated into recognizable tango form in Argentina. It was a 'low' dance, danced in brothels and in the street and commonly by 'Negroes'. What's distinctive about tango is that it actually crossed economic and racial lines on a regular basis: black men visiting the brothels were actually allowed to dance, in public for the first recorded time, with white women. Upwardly mobile landowners would dance on the same floor as ex-slaves, and often men would dance with other men. It was a deeply scandalous dance, something most upper-class Argentinians, along with lesbianism and infanticide, wouldn't even admit existed. Most important, and perhaps dangerously from the upper classes' perspective, tango obliterated social lines. What scandalized the upper classes was not the sexual metaphor of tango, but the identity of those partaking in the metaphor. Sex in many forms is an effective way of reiterating clearly marked structures of power, but somehow the tango, uniquely, avoided this. Even if it was only for those brief moments on the dance floor, tango actually equalized partners, no matter what their sex, race, or class.

I didn't know this at first. Before I ever started tango, I had decided it was a sexist dance. But in truth, in my lessons with Ivan especially, these things hardly seemed to do with his being a man. Acting out the Hegelian theory of the enslaved master, Ivan depended upon my following even more than I did upon his leading, and my most persistent mistake was in anticipating his next move. The first lesson he stopped more than a dozen times, put my arms down for me, stepped back, and looked straight at me with those beguiling eyes: 'No, no. You're not listening to me. You don't know how to just wait and listen.'

He got that much right. I thought of all the men in my life who at one point or another – standing in their doorway in jeans, naked in my living room, in their silk ties on their way to work – telling me the same thing. It surprised me, you know: I always thought I'd *like* being lead, like taking no responsibility for the course of things. I like taking control when I'm adept, there being few pleasures quite so exquisite as being elegant at something, but I'm always just a little bit more happy to be passive. Still, there are a lot of rules, a lot of boundaries. And yet, somehow, I'd never anticipated *this*; the slight sweat I could feel through Ivan's shirt, and, as silly as it sounds, just how close he'd stand next to me.

I remember when I was finally relieved of my burdensome virginity. I'd pictured the event a million times in my head, had read a score of writings about it, looked at a hundred photos, yet somehow the actual, tactile fact of having to part my legs so wide surprised me. It was morning and the light was coming in and his cats were sitting on the floor idly watching us. Their hair floated in a thin line of early sun. Unaccustomed to such a position, my left hip suddenly cracked loudly into the silence. Embarrassed by the volume, I looked up at him, my first lover, a new, small island of doubt forming in an already large sea of doubt.

At each of my private weekly lessons, I try to drop little asides to Ivan about my exciting, fascinating life.

'I can deduct all this, you know, because I'm a writer. I'm going to write about tango.'

'You must your feet more quickly in the turn move,' he replies.

'Of course, I might have to miss my lesson next week

because I'm waiting to hear from my agent if I have to fly to Burma.'

'Perhaps it is time for shoes with proper leather soles for you to buy. These boots you always wear, they are for a boy on a farm, not for tango!'

In the group lessons my fellow fledgling men practically demand that I lead, for they have no idea how to maintain a proper frame. Here, quite unlike the ideal Ivan, I am thoroughly disgusted by the general and everyday reality of most men's ineptitude. It is no wonder, I think, that I don't know how to listen. Ivan *knows* how to hold me. Here, in group class, I find myself forcing the correct space between myself and my random partners, pressing them too hard simply so that they will resist and thus create at least a portion of the correct tension required to hold me. This inexperience, combined with the predictable routine of steps required for such clumsy practice, not only accentuates but fosters my desire to be in control. This only ruins me worse for the private lesson. Initially, Ivan simply tells me when I'm not listening to his signals, but as the weeks wear on he takes a more definitive form of action: When I don't listen, he physically pushes me away. We stand there for a moment, squared off, the other couples in the large space spiraling past us.

While I was watching the Addams family tango, I had no idea that I was also watching a cultural fall-out of tango in the worst, bourgeois capitalist terms. To understand this, you have to look at another popular TV family closely related to the Addamses: the Munsters. The Munsters, you see, unlike the Addamses, were working-class: Herman Munster worked as manual laborer in a cemetery, while his wife, Lily, was the quintessential housewife, commonly seen performing domestic chores, though usually with a twist, as when she dusted by actually spraying dust on the furniture. In contrast, the Addamses were infinitely wealthy. Gomez was always spending millions at the drop of a hat, and there were continual references to gold mines and trunks filled with jewels. Often, Gomez, who had a number of university degrees, could be seen reading a stock market ticker tape: when he lost one fortune it was greeted with a casual shrug, suggesting there was plenty more where that came from.

Unlike Lily, Morticia was never seen preforming menial tasks: she wore a binding black dress that would have prevented any such effort anyway, a dress that also happened to be based on a style made popular in the early 1900's by tango dancers. The Munsters, who never once tangoed, were lower middle class and bore a physical freakishness they could not escape, or could ever wish to escape, since it was always crucial to the plot that they consider themselves as adhering to the norm. The Addamses, on the other hand, were decidedly upper class. Though the immediate family, the two parents and the two children, chose to be surrounded by freaks, they themselves were physically normal: their freakishness was based instead on eccentricities carried to the extreme, eccentricities supported by Gomez's boundless wealth and ego.

The point of all this is that the tango itself was just another dance in the global scheme of things until it got taken up by the French in the early 1900's. To the cultural imperialists of that era all exotics served the same function: to amuse a class of people at the same time it solidified their economic and social position. Traveling shows of 'exotics' showed men dressed as gauchos preforming the salacious tango. In reality, gauchos had little to do with tango, and to have them equated with it was not only historically incorrect, but as absurd as something else often featured in these shows of foreign exotics – African-Americans dressed up as American Indians. It didn't actually matter to the Europeans that someone had gotten it wrong, because any gradation of social or cultural importance that didn't directly relate to their class was highly inconsequential. And so it was with tango. It was a 'low' dance that offered the thrill of slumming, and if its intricate social importance was obliterated by the good times, no one particularly noticed or cared.

Tango became all the rage, sweeping its way across Europe during the 1910's and 1920's. And then, with the brand of bourgeois respectability placed upon it by Europe, tango was redefined for Argentina, and somehow became the dance of choice. Tango's golden age in Argentina, which lasted from about 1930 to 1955, was fueled by the dubious nationalism of Juan Perón, who wanted to regain Argentina's national pride, yet wanted to regain that pride by making Argentina appear as European as possible. For Perón, who pushed the tango as a dance of cultural identity, tango represented the perfect tool of propaganda. It has a history far too complicated to contain and thus easy to forget, and an allure far too seductive to dismiss.

After my first six-week lesson cycle was over, I talked the man I was seeing into taking classes with me. I was sure it would save our relationship. Because he'd never danced, he had to take the first-level classes, and I opted to take them again with him, something the instructors generally encouraged. This was a mistake. Stephen has what my students call a 'white boy' way of dancing, which, in his defense, I like to think is the result of his listening to a lot of acid rock during the 1970's. What really shocks me though isn't Stephen's lack of rhythm, but my impatience with him. Me? I'd always thought I was the perfect lover, the perfect partner. All those years of loneliness it never occurred to me that *I'd* have trouble loving someone, only that I'd have trouble finding someone to love me. Yet, here on the dance floor with someone who loved me, I found myself turning into what I'd always referred to as a bitch.

'No, no, no,' I'd tell him, trying to shove his hand on to the right place on my back. When he wouldn't hold me with enough tension, I'd let my body collapse against his, causing him to trip. Often, I considered slapping him. Sometimes, as the music played and we practiced our steps, I'd catch a glimpse of us in the huge wall mirror: with Stephen's tall good looks and my tiny figure we made a pretty good-looking couple, but I couldn't let it rest, immediately I'd start picking apart what was wrong with his head position, whinily insist he hold my hand up higher. In retrospect, I'm amazed he never slapped me.

For all its emphasis on machismo, tango is one of the unsung heroes of the modern feminist movement. Both upper-class and bourgeois European women of the early 1900's not only left the house unaccompanied, something unheard of only a few years before, they actually allowed complete strangers to hold them so immodestly at the *Thés Dansants* that were becoming all the rage across Europe. Women also used these tea dances as arenas for experiments in smoking in public, as well as to show off shocking fashions that revealed their natural shapes. Well-bred matrons were known to swoon at the very sight of a sex-laden tango. *Except* . . . the original scandal of tango, back in the slums of Argentina, had to do with its class and race relations; once Europe co-opted it, the scandal was transferred to its erotic content, and once that happened, it was ready to become a product. Tango started appearing in film and in plays and by virtue of this alone converted into something viewed openly wicked yet privately desired. In other words, a highly salable product. The loud moanings of sex not only drowned out the more complicated cries of racial economics, it also shifted the scruples of tango into a new, and far less threatening, form. The historical result of prohibiting sex has been to make it seem even more desirable, and the beauty of that, from the imperialist's point of view, lies in that the circle of tango's desire was now closed far more neatly and self-sufficiently than if it had been allowed to retain its original, far more unpredictable sins related to money and skin color.

Once, I got stuck in the airport for a few hours with a man I was interested in. We looked through magazines to pass the time and inevitably found ourselves taking the 'how much do you know about sex?' quiz in *Cosmopolitan.* When he answered the question, 'How many orgasms can a woman have in one session of lovemaking?' with C, four or less, I looked at him in shock. Didn't he know? Men own 99 per cent of the world's real estate and rake in 78 per cent of its earnings, despite the fact they only account for 44 per cent of its work force. Didn't he know the one sure thing women have to lord over men? When I answered, E, unlimited, my friend wouldn't believe me and we almost fought about it, until I forced him to look up the answers in the back of the magazine. We sat there quiet for a few moments, a silence filled with his embarrassment, and then a whole group of stewardesses passed by us, pulling their compact luggage on squeaking wheels past a giant rubber tree, their tight, luridly colored pants matching the carpet they walked on, decorated with the airline's infantile logo. My friend's eyes watched their back ends as they walked away from us. I watched him watch them, and then he looked back at me and somehow now, inexplicably and perhaps unjustly, the embarrassment was mine.

Months later, after too many drinks, we ended up in bed, and we both remembered. He dared me. I lay back while he watched and I set to work, just to prove something. After more than he was untroubled by, he started accusing me of faking it, so we quit. Something uncomfortable had happened between us, but why didn't we know how to say it, how to stop it, or, for that matter, how to keep it going? It had stopped being pleasurable early on, but I kept thinking I had to prove it, prove it, prove it. Prove what?

The truth is that I never did get Ivan to give me a glance even remotely colored by desire. The truth is that I never did become a particularly good tango dancer. I wanted the emotion, the passion, but I balked at the work.

At the end of what was to be our final lesson together, Ivan broke all my illusions. He took me into his office and sat me down.

'Do you want some coffee, some tea?' he asked.

It was the first time he'd ever not rushed off to his next student at the end of lesson, usually leaving me feeling slightly awkward and abandoned there in the school's hallway. A wind of hope breezed through me as he leaned intimately forward to tell me something.

'This, as you may remember, is the end of your first six-week lesson cycle.' His accent tangled the consonants. 'You would like to buy the next cycle, yes?'

I looked at him, half amused, half tired of the whole thing. I felt vaguely guilty, vaguely ashamed. There is no way to buy passion. Just as tango was watered down politically before being handed back to the Argentineans, its erotic content had been co-opted by and for the Europeans who 'discovered' it. In rigidly defined cultures such as early nineteenth-century Europe, passion is a dangerous thing, best kept corseted. Tango promised its European practitioners scandal, but it did so in a highly predictable manner. It offered the thrill and illusion of participating in a culture unburdened by civilized conventions, but it did so within the tight confines of money. It seemed to escape the dancers' notice that they had to pay to enter the dance-halls, had to buy the numerous fashions which became all the rage, had to book well-paid instructors weeks in advance, had to begin to worry if they would be invited to the 'right' tango party.

In Ivan's office, poorly framed posters hung askew on the walls: exotic, passionate poses of men bending dramatically and sexually over limber, provocative women, the costumes all 1970's-style sequins and the makeup and hair pushed to an unnatural extreme. I knew now that these poster poses came from competition tango, which is different from actual tango in that it is all choreographed, the dramatic poses all set up beforehand, all premeditated in their effect; they have little to do with the raw, unpredictable drama that surfaces unexpectedly when you dance tango freestyle.

'I'll take a check, if you want?' he asked, hopefully.

FOOL IN BOOTS

IN THE PICTURE, A model is sitting on a very white and expensive-looking carpet, looking dreamily at a spot just somewhere off to the side. She is wearing a black turtleneck, khaki-colored pants, and a pair of exquisitely made riding boots. A deep and grainy brown color, the boots are to die for, the whole purpose of this advertisement. I can almost smell the peaty, nostalgic fragrance of the delicate leather as it envelopes her slim calves and folds around her ankles in creases so supple I want to reach out and run a finger, a whole palm, along that soft, sturdy lushness. I don't even want to know how much they cost, but I'm certain that if I had a pair of boots like that, I'd be the coolest thing going.

The strange thing, though, is that I *have* a pair of boots almost like them. As I sit here writing this, I must confess that these boots are sitting at the bottom of a – shall we say 'strewn'? – closet, gathering not just dust but, yes, I'll admit it, mold, because I never properly cleaned the horse sweat off them from the last time I rode in them. They need new soles desperately, are scarred around the toes where the leather has torn and been resewn, and the color is fading on the inside calves from years of rubbing against so many saddles and lathering animals. I absolutely adore them. They represent years of dependable service, and though I do occasionally venture out in them in nonequestrian settings, this is only when I want to hang out with my bohemian downtown clique of friends, when I want to go *against* established fashion trends.

Another thing that struck me about the magazine ad, after the initial desire to possess the boots, was the fact that the model was sitting on a white carpet. One thing I can guarantee you about *my* boots is that they haven't been invited on to too many white carpets, especially expensive white carpets. My boots actually get used for what they were made for, meaning they spend a lot of time walking about in mud and manure and, as a result, don't look quite as good, not nearly as fashionable, as the boots in the magazine. My guess, and I may be wrong, but my guess is that anyone who lays out the money for those other boots will not be bringing their investment into contact with dirty barn floors anytime too soon. For if those boots were to be used functionally, if they were to fulfill the destiny their whole design is historically based upon, they'd be ruined for this other more ephemeral (and more expensive) purpose of fashion.

Riding boots are just one example of how clothes designed to perform specific jobs in the world can become fashionable and, the more fashionable they become, the more useless they grow in regard to that original function. It's as if design comes to eclipse the thing that gives rise to it in the first place: The humble bumpkin grows into a city slicker and leaves his small town behind. If that bumpkin is lucky, he'll beguile all the girls with that folksy charm none of them can know is the very thing, in its purest form, that he wanted to leave behind.

Another horsey case in point is jodhpurs, or riding breeches. Over a decade ago, street-smart girls starting buying old breeches from thrift stores, heavy-clothed and usually boot-polish-stained cast-offs from the wealthier classes. In their imaginative ways, these women started wearing them to clubs, placing them in contexts their original makers and owners could never could have foreseen. By re-inventing the breeches' original purpose, these women turned a functional design that only a decade or two before reeked of stodginess into something terribly cool.

If one spotlights the point that these breeches originally belonged to wealthy upper-class people, then a decade ago the thrifty, nonexclusive appropriation of the design into street wear can be viewed as decidedly political. Yet now, after fashion designers have diligently, wisely, and lucratively looked to what is happening small-time on the streets for inspiration toward the next big-time trend, breech-style pants and leggings can be seen in abundance. Whether in flimsy cotton interpretations found at a street vendor, or in high-priced silk versions sold in Bloomingdale's and Barneys, there are all these people walking around city streets looking ready to mount up.

Except, of course, that most of these people have never been within a dozen feet of a horse. How could they, then, know that these fashionable breeches would never work if you actually tried to wear them on a horse? They'd bunch up at the knee, the calf seams would pull in the wrong direction, the seat would be ruined in moments. Crucial functional elements of the original design have slowly evolved, in the hands of designers who either forgot or never knew how those designs related to a specific function, into elements of style. You can't use it any more, but it looks better than ever.

Riding clothes caught my attention because, as a longtime rider, they're something I know about. But once I started thinking about this process of how functional clothes become fashionable, I was startled to see just how common this process is in the industry. Remember when bicycle shorts caught on a few years ago? I recall my bicycle-racer friend Gil standing in a store, doubtfully picking off of the rack a fashionable version of the shorts he always associated with sweat, dirt, and effort. He held them up, felt the rough inner seams with his finger, and laughed. 'Anyone who tried wearing these on a bicycle would be *very* sorry and *very* sore.'

Right now the big thing happening along this wavelength is motorcycle boots. All these people walking around in these rather kinky calf-high lace-up boots that were born (and how many of the people wearing them know this?) of The Hog. Men started out with their own version of the black blunt-toed boot with the little leather strap around the ankle. The leather strap was for reinforcement and fitting purposes, the blunt toe made partly from cobbler ease (cheaper and easier to make), and partly so that they wouldn't be confused with pointy-toed cowboy boots.

Back in the 1950's, motorcycle riders strived to be outlaw rebels, while cowboys were the cultural symbol of the old, conservative, hick America; motorcyclists shuddered at even the thought of anyone thinking the word *cowboy* and *motorcycle* in the same instance. Now that this bit of cultural history has been lost, those of us who are neither members of a motorcycle gang nor particularly good at lassoing don't understand the disparity of wearing a motorcycle jacket with cowboy boots. There's just something about leather and little jangly bits that apparently makes people feel tough, and that's good enough for them.

Now, in the present, just to wear these things and know only that you feel cool does appear to be enough to justify the act. So what if you're a girl who never actually rides on the back of a motorcycle and thus does not actually need calf-high boots so as not to burn yourself on the exhaust pipe? How could you ever know that the high-heel and platform version of these boots would be not only useless but downright dangerous if you really did try to use them for the purpose they were originally made for? In essence, anyone who knows the history, who understands the use behind these things, instantly recognizes the absurdity of the fashion version of these clothes, while most others, ignorant of history and origin, buy them up in droves.

Probably the best-known example of functional clothes that became fashionable are blue jeans. Although there'd been various versions of it around already, blue jeans are mostly credited to having been invented during the Gold Rush of the 1880's and 1890's. They were invented out of desperation, actually: No other pants lasted long enough out there in the mines and field. For the longest time, blue jeans were something only the lower class wore. This started changing during World War II, when there were shortages of cloth and a lot of people doing physical labor. Then the 1950's brought all those motorcycle rebels mentioned earlier, and wearing jeans actually became a statement. You were working class, or at least sympathetic to the working class, and proud of it. This process evolved in the 1960's, when making such 'political statements' became fashionable. You could only buy the hard, dark blue jeans then, and people used to sit around washing them twenty times in a row, running them over with trucks, even burying them in their backyards for a few months, all to get that genuine look. Except of course what was transpiring was that rather than actually doing the work the jeans were built for, people were happy to take shortcuts and attain the *appearance* of having worked in their jeans. The middle classes liked being one with the working classes so long as it involved a minimum of work. It wasn't what you did in your jeans, their function, which mattered now, was their defining quality, now it was what they said both about and for you which became their purpose. Fashion designers caught on, and thus the terrible, dark age of stone-wash commenced, or, if you were a bit more subtle, the age of pre-shrunk, pre-frayed jeans; market-driven-priced jeans that, in essence if not in symbol, embodied their purchasers' willingness to purchase someone *else's* work and to be admired for this. For a long time, in fact, you could buy jeans only with that worn-in look; the original dark and stiff version practically went out of existence. Then, recently, true to the old truism, the original dark jeans got so old they became new again, and both The Gap and Levi's have been selling dark, stiff blue jeans that their advertising campaigns like to associate with that multi-use word, *tradition*.

Fashion *depends* upon a very rarified type of knowledge and a very broad type of ignorance. There are a lot of different definitions of fashion, but the one I like most is that an item becomes fashionable when its worth grows out of proportion to its actual production value. More extremely, the fashionable element of a fashion item is that element which is utterly without function or use outside of appearing fashionable. The two most simple ways to get people to buy something that is essentially useless is to count on the fact that they will not understand the history behind the object (if the history is understood the object risks appearing ridiculous), and to rely upon the historical truth that the complex relationship between form and function is easily severed by the intricacies of the modern world, intricacies honed even sharper by the endemic lack of curiosity about such matters.

Meanwhile, in a turnabout so extreme it's got to be profound, it's the very *knowing* about fashion that is so highly valued by us. To know what is fashionable before it becomes 'common' is a knowledge highly praised and rewarded. The role of desire is switched; it is no longer, as most religions and philosophies tell us, about being led *away* from our true selves. In the realm of fashion, desire *becomes* the self, or at least the stand-in for it, and who and what we are (and, perhaps more important, who and what we are *not*) is now definable by what we can recognize as fashionable. The more 'high' our desire, the higher we must be; the more original our tastes, the more special we must be, and the more expensive our needs, the more valuable we must be.

You know the really sad part? Knowing all this, I *still* want those damned boots.

THE COUNTRY OF CHILDHOOD

I WAS FORCED INTO becoming an American citizen in my early thirties. My publisher wanted to submit work of mine for a prize, but only afterward did anyone read the fine print: only U.S. citizens were eligible. I called the prize committee to confirm; my thirty-year-old green card status meant nothing. I had to be a *bona fide* citizen. I'd lived in this country for all but four years of my life, but I did *not* want to become a citizen. Why? The best answer might be to say that though technically I am an immigrant from another country, a truer thing to say might be that I immigrated from a myth. Let me try to explain.

My family left Ireland for America when my twin sister and I were only four, after my father, a journalist, was offered a job in New York. Though I have lucid and muscular memories of Ireland, they are still a child's memories; pictures of unnarrated events punctuated with stark details and odd choices of focus – the penguin's beak poking through the bars in the Dublin Zoo, the moss on the stone wall outside our house, the soft triangular ears of the spotted dog that belonged to some blurry neighbor.

Ireland, however, was the locus of my family's first migration; some seven years before arriving in Dublin they'd lived in England, my mother's homeland. Though my father was Irish, and my sister Sarah and I were Irish, everyone else in the family was actually English. Such gradations of geography did not matter to the Americans, however, once we arrived there in 1969, after our second migration. The Americans interchanged the two countries out of ignorance, Sarah and I did so out of instinct; both places were important parts on the family map, and we'd just as likely respond with either when asked where we were from.

Sarah and I occupied last place in the family lineage. Sean was so much older, thirteen years, that he was both technically and metaphorically a stranger by the time I could string my days together eloquently enough to live them in linear time, when I was perhaps around seven. This is precisely when he left home for good, to go live in California, three thousand miles away. I saw him only once more, when I was eleven or so, before he died in a road accident.

Nicholas was only three years younger than Sean, but more inclined to stay at home, and he took over the role of older brother after Sean left. Suellen was comparatively young, only three years younger than Nick, but six years older than Sarah and I. It was quite obvious to all concerned that Sarah and I were mere infants without rights, while Susie and Nick were adults. They perpetuated this idea, claiming adult privileges of bedtimes and food choices and tempers and any-show-they-wanted on the television. Sarah and I perpetuated this hierarchy also, because anything they said we automatically assumed to be more important than anything we said, or could even possibly imagine saying.

And they had a lot to say. My older siblings did not like America, and they particularly hated Americans; part of their arguments were viable, but a large part of their contentions, I recognized only later, were tempered by the anger endemic to all teenagers and, in particular, teenagers who have been forceably relocated. 'America is an *awful* place,' they told us repeatedly, in a wide variety of contexts. They said bad things about the States with an inventive zeal that bordered on fondness. After all, their distaste was tempered by a poorly disguised nostalgia. As they spewed on and on in scandalized tones about how *bourgeois*, how *tacky* and *vulgar* Americans were (despite the fact these last two terms were invented by the bourgeoisie), my older siblings had a clear picture of what they were comparing the States with.

Sarah and I, however, were on the other side of this European door, and the only thing we could see through this door was the hated thing itself. We had no solid memory of the country that came before, only images that belonged as much to the country of childhood as to any literal map.

'American television is so *vapid*,' Nicholas announced after walking by and seeing me sitting on the floor in front of the television. There was a reasonably good chance I was enjoying whatever it was I was watching – television enthralled me as a child – and all I could do was wonder what personal defect made me enjoy it so. How profound, how intricate, how enlightening Irish and English television must be. The fact that I couldn't understand at all the appeal of *Upstairs, Downstairs* on public television was only one more mark against me, I reasoned.

My Irish accent was ironed out of me by the time I was nine or so, though it occasionally makes sporadic appearances depending on to whom I'm speaking. But growing up I towed the family line and believed fully that I was not an American. Every year on St. Patrick's Day I scoffed at all these silly Americans wearing green and claiming to be Irish. 'Real Irish people don't give a damn about St. Patrick's Day.' And I was right; to focus on it so is an American trend. Years later, I met a woman who said, 'I'm Italian,' and I was shocked. 'But you speak English so well,' I said, and was laughed at. Of course she did; she was born in New York, as were her parents.

National identity, to many Americans, includes the claiming of another country as one's own.

It was summer the day I had to make the choice to become a legal American. Only my father had ever actually become a citizen (Susie and Nick returned as adults to live in London), and only my sister Sarah understood my reluctance. My publisher, however, did not. Finally, partly because a Republican was in office and changing immigration laws (it was not inconceivable I would lose certain rights; terrible stories were circulating) and partly because I wanted the option to return to live in Europe and then return to live in America if I wished (something you can't do legally on a green card), I called the Immigration and Naturalization Services' 800 number. I was at a writers' colony at the time and had to cramp into a sweltering phone booth. The automated service listed dozens upon dozens of options (I hung up after the voice told me 'press 29') including the option ('press 14', I think it was) to report an illegal alien. It dawned on me that this might be quite a process.

While growing up, foreign goods sometimes appeared in the kitchen; Irish sausages and Cadbury chocolate, Weetabix for breakfast, or bright cardboard tubes of Smarties after dinner if we were good. It's not that I didn't love these foods (even I could recognize the superiority of Cadbury over Hershey), but they were talismans from a mythic 'olden days' when the general state of family affairs had been better than it was here in America. Things were not going well on this side of the big pond; garrulous money problems, a generally bruised outlook tendered by illness and unemployment, a deepening sadness that became the background rhythm of daily life. I felt I'd missed out on the earlier, better times of the family (I accepted *a priori* that they had been better) simply by being born too late. America was the land of our discontent, I was told repeatedly, and the luminous appeal of nostalgia, a nostalgia for something I knew only in the abstract, began to haunt me.

Nostalgia. Who has not fallen for its wiles? Advertising companies use it blatantly: sepia pictures of old men on bicycles, delivering bread; whisky distillers inviting us to 'share the tradition'; catalog companies perfectly mimicking the styles and slang of a long-dead generation. Politicians coax it out of us too: 'old-fashioned values' and 'a return to strength' as acceptable campaign promises. But note that the modus operandi of these examples is a nostalgia for an unclear, or even nonexistent past. To long for the past is a very human thing, but what does it say about us when we long for a past we never actually participated in? And when we do long for the specific, it seems that any event is up for grabs; it's not uncommon for people to become nostalgic for what were objectively difficult, even miserable times of their lives.

In Gabriel García Márquez's *One Hundred Years of Solitude*, there is a learned bookstore owner known simply as 'the wise Catalonian'. He's an important figure toward the end of the book because he becomes the sole protector of real-world wisdom in a town that is falling inexorably into a world of loss and forgetfulness. The wise Catalonian is the last holder of insight and erudition, despite the fact he spends most of his time in the doomed town of Macondo wistfully wishing he were back in his hometown on the Mediterranean. And yet, when he finally does return to his original home, he finds himself missing Macondo.

> 'One winter night while the soup was boiling in the fireplace, he missed the heat of the trees, the whistle of the train during the lethargy of siesta time, just as in Macondo he had missed the winter soup in the fireplace, the cries of the coffee vendor, and the fleeting larks of springtime. Upset by the two nostalgias facing each other like two mirrors, he lost his

> marvelous sense of unreality and he ended up recommending to all of them that they leave Macondo, that they forget everything he had taught them about the world and the human heart, that they shit on Horace, and that wherever they might be they always remember that the past was a lie, that memory has no return, that every spring gone by could never be recovered, and that the wildest and most tenacious love was an ephemeral truth in the end.'

One of the many things I watched on television as a child in the bright, endless, almost viscous space of the weekends were old movies made in England, mostly black-and-white mysteries and romances. Meanwhile, in color, I could watch documentaries on public television, *Monty Python's Flying Circus*, any other number of 'grown up' shows I didn't always get. But what I was watching for was not the content of the shows and movies themselves, but the details, the background: the always wet streets, the phone boxes, the door handles, the teapots, the road signs, the stone walls and hedges; – the million details of daily life that are the true separators between cultures. All these details accumulated and came to represent a parallel world that very quickly became abstract. It's not exactly that I doubted such a landscape existed; it's that I automatically confused what was on television with what couldn't possibly be real, simply because it *was* on television.

I left America for several years in my twenties; I lived in Berlin, London, and Scotland, while visiting other countries as well. (How I was able to return to this country in my early thirties after three years abroad is a story I can't confess to in print.) One Sunday in Paris, before my return to the States, I read an astute observation by an ex-pat in *The International Herald Tribune*; America is like death: everything we ever learn about life is discovered in the process of trying to escape it. It was true; I only really learned to *see* America once I left it. And the fact that I even call it *America* was, I learned, itself a symptom. There is no such country as America, my European friends corrected me; America is a continent, not a country. It is only Americans themselves who forget its real name: the United States of America.

What did I learn about America while living away from it? First, that no matter how much I wished to see myself as a non-American while growing up, I was acutely American. I possessed the very sense of entitlement I'd accused others of, an entitlement that came across subtly in the fact that I spoke only English, and embarrassingly in that when I first arrived in Europe I genuinely believed others would be interested in me simply and only because I was from America. I lacked a very basic set of inner coordinates, a map with properly drawn boundaries.

On a smaller level, the level of details, I found myself missing American things. I became fanatical about finding Reese's Peanut Butter Cups, and I avidly watched American programs on TV, programs I probably would have never watched if living in the States. Living in Europe, I was surrounded by the very details of European life that I'd held suspended in the halcyon amber of nostalgia my entire childhood, and now my two nostalgias, as they did for the wise Catalonian, mirrored each other. And it's not that I came to see that what I had pined for all my childhood (that life was better in Europe, that people were smarter, kinder) was untrue (because I do believe Europeans are better educated than Americans, and that education does create an arguably 'better' society on a number of levels), but that I recognized something much more personal in the endless repetition of images; there is always something to want, a place we would all rather be than where we are. Though I may have a very complex relationship to America, I can no longer, with any degree of self-honesty, dislike it simply because it is the place where I am.

The most inevitable and frustrating part of becoming a citizen of the United States of America is waiting in lines. Simply to enter into the INS building in downtown New York takes several hours, and all that happens once you get in is that you get to wait on more lines. But, I was acutely aware, I was white (blond-haired and blue-eyed to boot) and I spoke fluent English. It was immediately understood that I would have no trouble getting my papers, and that it was only the tediousness of the process that was the obstacle. That this should be so angered me, and made the self-motivated skepticism behind my decision to become a citizen (which I freely admitted) that much stronger.

Before taking your 'test' as part of the naturalization process (which includes knowing what Congress does and being able to write in legible English *I promise to be a good citizen*) prospective citizens have to wait in an obscenely boring and decrepit waiting room. The only decoration in this windowless room is a group of drawings made by a second-grade class that had obviously visited the INS on some field trip. Wobbly Statue of Liberties and out-of-proportion American flags hung by triangles of Scotch tape on their corners. There was a whole series of drawings that were outlines of small hands – exactly like the traced hands I was taught to make Thanksgiving turkeys out of in grade school – with each finger named Liberty, Justice, Freedom, and Equality (the thumb, oddly, had no name). Then each whole hand, colored with red, white, and blue crayons, was identified as the United States of American by virtue of a carefully drawn title on the top or bottom of the paper. How fitting, I thought with my inherited cynical air, that here in this room it is the childish, simplistic view of America that prevails, a view manufactured by rote and under adult supervision.

When the papers finally came through informing me of when and where to show up for the final ceremony, I treated it as a joke. What a lark, I thought, all for a silly prize I didn't even get. Almost a whole year had passed since that first phone call to the INS, and the prize had been awarded, meanwhile, to someone else. Also meanwhile, my brother, who'd been living abroad a few years, tried to return to America and was turned away; he'd simply been gone for too long. It would behoove me, I saw, to stick with it and have dual citizenship (though the U.S. does not recognize dual citizenship, Ireland does, and I travel with both passports).

My letter informed me I had to wear formal attire, which was odd, seeing as the ceremony was at nine o'clock in the morning. I put on a black cocktail dress (it was too hot to wear anything long), invited my boyfriend (himself a Canadian), rode the subway with all the commuters in my odd garb, and showed up exactly on time.

The building had a huge lobby, and they were not quite ready for us in the auditorium, so my fellow soon-to-be citizens and I waited en masse. There were about two hundred of us all together, plus at least two hundred family members there to cheer us on. The costumes and the colors were resplendently intricate and liquid; the flow of fabrics and details from all over the globe were not just dazzling, but moving. Along with the many 'American'-clad people (and do not think that there is not an American national costume) such as myself, national costumes from Africa, Asia, and Eastern Europe made not just their wearers but all of us that much more gorgeous.

When we were shepherded into the auditorium and sat down in rows, I began to hear the sound of weeping around me. There were many many reasons we all filled those rows that morning, and there were just as many emotional landscapes. I had been taking it for granted that everyone else saw this whole thing, as I did, as a charade, as a major inconvenience. Somehow, beforehand, I had thought we would all understand this was just a silly, bureaucratic, even propaganda-laced ceremony – but, no, I saw now how meaningful this was to some. Though it is not hard to make me feel ashamed, there is shame that only ratchets up the present degree of self-involvement, and then there is instructive shame. I felt ashamed of myself for having so underestimated the emotional power of the act of becoming a citizen, ashamed that I had underestimated this power because I was, despite my artistic bohemian beliefs about my second-class status, a deeply privileged person, if, once again, only because I was white and educated. As much as I understand the danger of defining privilege as something endemic to America (because it is so much more complex than such a simple reduction), as I sat there I understood that there are extraordinary things about America, and I was ashamed because I realized that it had been my very privilege in regard to my access to America that had blinded me to what those privileges entailed.

At the end of the ceremony, which included pledging allegiance to the flag (which I'd refused to do in high school), taking the oath of allegiance (I hadn't known there *was* an oath of allegiance), hearing a speech or two, and ritualistically handing in our green cards, a woman I recognized from the INS offices stepped forward to sing the National Anthem. The weeping grew louder around me as this woman sang this song so beautifully (this song I'd always laughed at before), and though it's almost embarrassing to say because it is so predictable, I actually loved America at that moment, if only because I saw how much these other people truly loved it, and because I could only guess at what they had been through to arrive at this love.

Still, when I am in America, I rarely feel completely American. When I am in Europe, I don't know what to feel. This is probably a good thing; uncertainty can be a privilege when one doesn't have to live in it all the time. Where I am now is more important to me than it used to be. Meanwhile, where I am from, whether that is Ireland or America or upstate New York or simply a place called the country of childhood, is harder to name now, an image that shifts all the time, wobbly and out of proportion, like any child's idea of what a country is.

MY GOD

MY EARLY RELIGIOUS EDUCATION, at the age of six, consisted of memorizing all the words to the rock opera *Jesus Christ Superstar*. Actually, I did more than memorize them, I acted out the whole album, my own private version of the musical. It was one of the few record albums my family brought over from Ireland when we moved to New York in the late 1960's. Combining my passion for this album with my crush on Mr Ed the talking horse, on whom I had one of those innocent crushes that couldn't distinguish between *loving* Mr Ed from wanting to *be* Mr Ed, I re-created the entire drama of Jesus and Judas and the twelve apostles as a talking horse. All this took place on a large yellow Chinese carpet that lay in front of the stereo in the living room. Each part of the carpet signified a character, and I'd canter on my hands and knees from corner to corner to mouth each part as it came up. Hired at great expense to the producers, my knees carpet-burning into a vivid red, I performed the entire drama singlehandedly. Naturally, people came from all over the globe to witness such a marvelous sight.

For the big chorus parts, I'd mount my Hippty-hop, a sort of big red rubber ball on which you could sit and then propel yourself by bouncing while holding on to a half-circle handle attached to the top. I'd race around the room, imagining that I was riding in complicated formation, banners flapping, as the apostles wondered what was happening, as the beggars and lepers overtook Jesus, as the crowd jeered, in harmony, for his crucifixion. The only drawback to the choruses was that my bouncing about often made the needle skip on the record, but it was also necessary as it gave my knees a short rest. It wasn't the performance that made me love the album; performing had to do with my courtship of the strong, safe, gleamingly visceral world of Mr Ed. I loved the album because music itself had an uncanny hold on me; the sways and turns of the emotional narrative entranced me even, and maybe especially even, when I didn't understand them. The pharisees were my favorites because their voices were so exotically varied, plus they all seemed so confused and put upon, which, even at six, was a state I identified with. I had to hold my ears during the scene in which Jesus was whipped by the forty-nine lashes, not because I felt bad for him, but because the music itself was so piercing and dreadful.

Not surprisingly, for the rest of my childhood, I held a rather liberal take on the New Testament. Jesus obviously possessed quite a number of very human failings, and though I knew from other sources, such as early-morning Sunday television, that he was a very kind person, he seemed fairly preoccupied a lot of the time in the gospel according to Andrew Lloyd Webber. I liked Judas far better, and felt sorry when he killed himself; in truth, he seemed like the only one with any deep feelings at all, and I thought he'd been unjustly set up. He also had a much better singing voice. This was all I knew, and even this I kept to myself. Religion, in my family, was regarded as a highly specialized form of stupidity.

A few years later, when I was about ten and very ill, I used to receive letters of 'hope and encouragement', from people I'd never met before, strangers who'd heard about my sad story and wrote in the hope of cheering me up. Each and every one of these letters eventually got around to God. Had I accepted him as my savior? How could these poor people ever guess the ridicule their letters received. My cynical older brothers, whose nasty humor I confused with worldliness, loved to read the letters out loud in the kitchen. Most of the letters were written in a rounded, overly even hand I'd learn to recognize more than a decade later, when I began teaching, as the generic handwriting of a dull education. My brothers, nine and thirteen years older than I, had been educated in Ireland, and their teachers had all been priests. At that point I don't think I'd ever actually met a priest, not face-to-face, and these letters caused my brother Nicholas to thicken and coarsen his accent, imitating specific priests he'd known. 'Have you accepted Jesus Christ as your savior, young girl?' he'd ask me in his strange voice, adding odd and specific physical tics – eyes that roamed leftward, hands that trembled – and this would push him over the edge into tearful hysteria. Left out of the joke, I could only pause and feel jealous, learning by osmosis that anyone who believed such things as these letters hinted at was a certifiable fool.

Except . . . there was a part of me that longed to believe. If I believed, then perhaps I'd be happy. My life at the time, due to my illness and the insanity endemic to my family, was outlined with and directed by every conceivable type of emotional, physical, social, and psychic bad luck. Luckily, my interior life was up for the job, and the world I inhabited, though by this time slightly less outwardly silly than pretending I was a talking horse playing out the New Testament, coursed like a fast stream over solidly built fantasies. I barely knew who I was, only who I pretended to be: a pony express rider, a space alien, an unrecognized genius, all of us flailing around in the white water of a desperate escape.

Some of the letters contained pamphlets. I'd sit at the

kitchen table, the cats rubbing around my legs, and read stories of saintly people who were able to bear any hardship, whether it was illness, solitude, poverty, or the scorn of others, with a grace that actually shone from them in the illustrations – shards of light emanating from the believers' heads (depending upon the illustrators' skill) like either soft mists or awkward bolts. Everyone's eyes were blue. What affected me most was their unwavering calm, and I'd sit there in the kitchen and look up from these pamphlets at my mother, sitting at the other end of the table, smoking furiously, making piles of different bills and lists and papers, her kinetic anger trembling with its own life in her hands. My mother's anger at everyone and everything possessed her like a demon, making her life, as she herself often said, a living hell. She was probably aware, at times, what effect it had on ours, but most of the time she was too busy dealing with the tragedies that haunted our family or too busy stalking her own luminous sadness to ever to sit down and speak with these demons.

Often, the pamphlets quoted verses from the Bible. These, too, were almost always about forgiveness and love, peace, and eternal joy. This was about as close as I got to actually reading the Bible. I did try at one point, after finding one downstairs in the basement, a King James version. Starting with Genesis, I decided to try, as one of the pamphlets suggested, reading a page a day for a year. I got to the first string of begats and that ended that project. Meanwhile, what I had read seemed such a peculiar story. Why would God pick on the snake like that? I wondered. And why were women made in what seemed like an afterthought? And why did everyone for ever and ever have to suffer because of someone else's mistake, a mistake that, to me, didn't really seem so terrible after all? Though I'd heard that many people believed all of this as something that actually truly really happened, surely those people would have to be discounted as idiots. All I had to do was stand outside on the front lawn, listening to the complex screams of neighborhood children and to the vast songs of the birds to just simply *know* it couldn't have happened in such a way. But then, why *did* so many people believe this? And how did Jesus fit into this? From what I could understand about him he seemed a decent sort of fellow, so why did they kill him? And why (because I'd just been reading about it in history class) did people do something as horrible as the Crusades in his name? And back in Northern Ireland, all that mess, why did that have to happen?

And yet I still longed desperately to believe. How could I cross that line? Did God exist? I conducted experiments in my room. Sitting Indian style on my carpet, I'd not so much ask as announce, 'God, if you exist, prove it to me.' Sometimes I'd qualify this, suggesting he (and He was always a he) do something like perhaps change the color of the carpet, or maybe make the family dog, who'd recently died, appear panting and wagging in front of me. I wanted the resounding silence following my questions to be the answer, the proof that I didn't have to waste my time wondering about such things any more. Yet I also wanted so badly all that peace, all that joy and love.

I'd lie in bed at night and pretend I was a saint. Often, I was simply an egomaniac, but that didn't matter. In my fantasy life, I learned what it felt like to have infinite patience and wisdom. I healed the sick, especially the grotesquely sick, and helped the poor, especially the poor no one else noticed, and especially the ones who lived in terror of despots. I read books about the Holocaust and imagined how I'd be so graceful there that I'd withstand oppression with such nobility that the Nazis would be forced to stop in their tracks. In Vietnam and Cambodia and amid the famines of Africa, I was there too, helping the lost and injured and sad. In my real life, I hated myself for being petty and shallow, because, try as I might, I could only manage my transmutation into benign understanding for just moments at a time. Acts of charity – these I only seemed to manage with animals, and even with them, whom I loved so much, I was often experimentally cruel. And the humans immediately around me; they had griefs far subtler than abject poverty and leprosy, sorrows far too near and familiar, and all I could do was flee.

Vincent Van Gogh, in his letters to his brother, Theo, outlined a life filled with the tangible. Vincent loved to look, to touch, to smell, and to taste the world about him. Most of all, he loved to look, and then *feel*, with his hands grasping the charcoal or brush, what he had just seen. His hands roamed all over his mind, trying to decipher the different grains of thought and emotion, the thin line between the actual and the imagined, between light and the things he saw with light. Though he never lived to hear of either wave or particle theories of light, Vincent understood that one doesn't just simply 'see' a chair or table, but rather that one's eyes are actually caressed by the light that bounces off them. Color, while being the most visible thing we can know about a tree, is also created by that part of light that the tree has cast off. The tree absorbs all other light waves of color, welcomes them as part of itself; the green we see is the negative, the reflected-off reality it wants no part of. Where its definition of itself ends, our definition of it is just beginning.

Vincent often mentioned to his brother what he called a longing for the old, old story. The first time I read this, as a freshman in college, I had no idea he was referring to the story of Jesus. But I'd only just taken up writing poetry, and something about the sadness, the unidentifiable need, the repetitious movement toward something ancient, pricked at me. As I was just discovering the world of writing, I discovered it was the religion I'd been searching for all my life. That even such a short phrase as written by Vincent could elicit such ineffable feelings in me seemed miraculous. I'd spent most of my childhood using the small tactile details of the world as a way of escaping the world; how easy to separate myself from the shame and misery of certain moments when I could suddenly appreciate the texture of the carpet as a doctor paced on it, the dewlike drops forming on the glass of water in front of my angry mother, its reflected rim a hoop of light quivering on the table.

Writing offered a way to take these small observations and transform them into a way of entering the world, a way of using language as the slow tear in the safe fabric I'd been wrapping myself up in. My own particular tool was language, but I loved art of all kinds, particularly visual art. The concept of time seemed at the heart of all these arts. Art, to me, was anything that brought you into the present moment, the nameless now that keeps dying and being reborn over and over and over. That the present moment should be so nameless, so inexpressible, I believed was the fundamental truth of art, and I defined beauty as the thing left over from the effort of trying to name it. The painter Robert Henri said it best in a quote that, during the height of my artistic evangelism, probably my junior year, I memorized by heart: 'There are moments in our lives, there are moments in a day, when we seem to see beyond the usual. Such are the moments of our greatest happiness. Such are the moments of our greatest wisdom. If one but could recall this vision by some sort of sign. It was in this hope that the arts were invented. Signposts on the way to what may be. Signposts toward greater knowledge.'

My senior year in college I decided to take a course entitled 'The Bible as Literature'. I took it because of the literature part of the title. In my endless quest for metaphors, I thought it might help my writing. The first assignment, naturally enough, was to read Genesis. I admit I only skimmed the begats. By this time I knew enough about anthropology, ancient myths, and other world religions to recognize Genesis as a good story. For a few years previous I'd been dabbling with Eastern Religion, with a little Western Philosophy thrown in as well. More and more, I came to see that just as with art, the essence of the religious moment lay within the 'now' moment, and that the heinous clichés of the world were born in the belief that you could capture this moment. Once you judged, once you decided, you were closed off, locked into misinterpretations of the past and misapprehensions of the future. The more I looked at it, the more religion looked like art.

As we read more of the Old Testament, I was seized by a great crisis. The closer I read, the more shocked I was by my own previous ignorance of what was going on in the Bible. I guess I'd always thought it was all about love and joy and peace. The violence, the anger of the Old Testament terrified me simply by its presence, but the real terror lay in my having to acknowledge that the culture I lived in was based, in large part, upon this violent saga, a story as unfair as it was unforthcoming. That so many generations upon generations of people, that people living today, took this work to be the literal truth, deeply disturbed me. How could one be happy with such tautology, to simply be 'told' the meaning of everything, never allowed to question? And the entire drama of the story was based on God's will – all those humans forced into their roles – for it was God who hardened people's hearts, God who closed their eyes against the truth, God who selected only a chosen few, leaving the rest to annihilation, or worse. What could the purpose of life be if it was already laid out in such monotonous script?

Early in the Christian Era, Philo of Alexandria changed the course of history by being one of the first philosophers to undertake and, most important, to write about, an allegorical exegesis of a religious text later to be Hebrew Scripture. At that point in history the Library of Alexandria was being formed. Ships from the known world called into port there, and the rulers of the day made it law that all books upon these ships must be surrendered up to the State and copied into Greek; after translation, they were returned to their owners. It was during this time Jewish religious texts were translated into Greek, and it was this Greek translation that became the defining text for later Christians.

Up until the time of Philo, the text of the Bible was a kind of property, controlled by educated religious leaders and officials. The text itself was mysterious to those who could not read, and faith was contained in the act of believing in the stories. The stories either happened or they did not, and your spiritual life was made up of how strongly you believed in the stories, your ruin in how much you did not. It was a very physical, very visceral kind of belief, one that contended that the path to God's love lay within your ability to follow ritual and to control your body. Philo, a Jew, however, read the stories as allegorical. He wrote at length about the possibility that spirit and matter were separated, that belief was an act of the mind, not simply of the body. You could perform rituals till the very end, but none of that mattered if you didn't believe with your head and heart, if you didn't actually think.

Philo inserted a new dimension into the whole concept of belief. 'Truth', as he saw it, didn't exist in the stories themselves, in the words on the page, nor in the black-and-white world of absolute faith, but in the process of using the wit and judgment and intellect given to us by God in interpreting these words. Meaning, for Philo, and unlike for many of his contemporaries, occurred not on set planes but only during the shift between these planes. Later, of course, those different planes were all too firmly established, and rather than think for yourself, you could only move between meanings rigidly defined by the Church. Philo himself, freely interpreting with only his instinct and education to guide him, would have been seen as a heretic during any number of later inquisitions, despite the fact it was his philosophies that set the groundwork for them. Surely he could never have foreseen that once people were able to move past literal methods of judging what was to become the Bible, they would then cast their abstract *ideas* about the Bible in do-or-die terms, become willing to torture and kill those who did not accept their ideas of what the Bible *meant*.

Not surprisingly, the information that impressed me most in the Old Testament had been the use of time. If the Garden of Eden was timeless, then linear history began with the Fall. The Old Testament set up a very particular story, charted a very inexorable course. Within this history, which was one type of linear time, or narrative, there was a second story with an even more refined sense of linear time, and this was the story of the Covenant. On the simplest level, the Covenant was a deal made between God and the Jews. At the beginning of this deal, it was promised that once the narrative ran its course, once the string of prophecies came true, God would end History and bring his people to the promised land. This end was, paradoxically, to be a return to the beginning state, to a timeless, or eternal, paradise. As I understood it, this made time in the Bible cyclical as well as linear.

By sheer luck, I was reading Gabriel García Márquez's *One Hundred Years of Solitude* at the same time I was reading the New Testament. If my history of religion-bashing prevented me from a full marveling at the narrative and artistic genius behind the story of the Bible, I was at least free to marvel at how Márquez intermeshed cyclical with linear time, showing through images of magic-realism (images that would be defined miraculous in the Bible) how we could always be in the 'now', but that also the string of nows moved inevitably forward. Death, after all, was the one now moment that brought the inner and the outer life together: Even if you've denied every now moment in your life, you are still moving forward toward that final inevitable moment. Márquez did this again and again with images: a bedroom untouched by time even as the house fell into decrepitude around it, the blind Ursula able to act as if she saw, simply by knowing routines (time) so well. This same Ursula, the matriarch of the family, could also symbolically lift herself out of time, lift herself out of habits others were caught in, and find objects such as wedding rings others thought irrevocably lost. Márquez exemplified the paradox of cyclical and linear time with Ursula. The Bible did it with Jesus.

As a poet, I was struck by the sheer genius of Jesus as a narrative device, Jesus as the ultimate paradox. No wonder, I thought, this story has survived with such force, no wonder it's compelled so many. Again, it was the use of time that grabbed me. Of course, there were Jesus' sermons and parables themselves, which were beautiful and attractive for their gentle strength and wisdom, but I could find any number of similar stories and sayings anywhere else I chose to look. It was the way Jesus died that tied it all together, which brought poetic force to his teachings. In particular, it was the things Jesus said on the cross as he died, which, once I turned my whole life's experience toward interpreting these words, astounded me. In Luke, when Jesus says 'Father, forgive them, they know not what they do,' a way to approach this utterance is to look at what he does not say. He doesn't say, 'Father, forgive them because soon they'll understand what they've done and they'll be sorry.' This type of reasoning for forgiveness depends upon the passage of time; in a future moment, people will be forced to relive the past and have their present moment forever sullied by that past. He doesn't say, 'Father, forgive them because they are too stupid to understand what's going on and need to be pitied.' To say this would be to say that humans are incapable of awareness because of a lack or deficit; rather, they know not what they do because they are trapped in the present moment and so can't understand the historical significance of their actions. And he doesn't say, 'Father, forgive them, because they'll be judged later anyway.' This would imply a purely apocalyptic sense of time, living a string of now moments isolated from each other by stupidity, as opposed to a string of now moments linked together by awareness. If you believe your life's meaning and value will be decided in the future, independent of what you do or suffer now, then there is no possibility of having your present life acquire meaning through being aware of that future, for that decision, unlinked to the now, could only be haphazard and incomprehensible.

What Jesus does say is 'Father, forgive them, for they know not what they do.' This implies that while the present moment may be incomprehensible, there is still the possibility of forgiveness, which would instill meaning and order not just to that single moment of future forgiveness, but would also instill meaning into all past and present moments, even those moments which were lived in doubt and chaos.

This last type of living in time is crucial to the whole concept of Forgiveness and Redemption, so significant to Christianity. If the Father represents the eternal, then his ability to forgive action created by linear time is the ultimate fusion of cyclical and linear time. When Jesus says, in John, 'It is finished,' I don't think he means just his life or his crusade. It is the end of the Old Testament sense of history. The prophecy has come to pass and the violent cause-and-effect type of history embodied in the Old Testament is over; a new sense of time is now in place, a sense of time being both eternally present and eternally changing. All these incredibly complex ideas embedded in a few sentences. This is what terrified me.

Yet, obviously the old sense of history, of violent and unjust cause and effect, wasn't over with the crucifixion. If anything, the Church itself became responsible for a great deal more violence. But those things *could* be changed, I believed, at least on the personal level, by acting with compassion and unconditional love. History itself would remain in place, as violent as ever, but small transcendent acts of personal dignity and grace could be acted out regardless. In the face of chaos, one had to act as if order and meaning were possible, despite the fact one could never be absolutely sure; the tangible miracles of the carpet changing color or the resurrected dog were not going to be the guidelines of success. Rather, I too had to use a much more abstract, internal gauge of spiritual success, recognizing all the while the possibility that I might simply be fooling myself. I recognized this process as exactly the same pattern of attempting to capture something in words or on a canvas, knowing all along that one will ultimately fail to produce an objective, final, and fully satisfying definition of beauty. I knew the moments in art when I was convinced I had produced something beautiful were not only the moments in which I was most likely wrong, but that the whole notion of being 'convinced' was itself the seat of the problem. If paintings and poems were the signposts in art that reminded you again and again of your needs and beliefs rather than letting you get sucked into the abyss of your material failures, then the words and deeds of Jesus could work the same way.

Except . . . I didn't want to Believe, not with a capital B. I didn't want to turn into the type of person I'd regarded as stupid my entire life. But there it was again: Was I just being trapped by my own history, my own inability to let go of the past? It was as if I were sitting back on my childhood carpet, the smell of tomato sauce coming from the kitchen and the sounds of scraping pots, as I tried to appeal myself into a position of belief. Now, wasn't I supposed to just take the plunge, that proverbial leap? Was it even a matter of will at all? I spent days lying on my bed in my college dorm, staring out the window at the gutter hanging down from the roof in the foreground, the top of an oak tree in the middle ground where large flocks of noisy starlings congregated each dusk, and the sky beyond.

I was taking chemistry at the time, and in lab each small group was handed little vials of an unknown substance. Our task was to determine what it was. In order to do this, we went through a series of tests, tests that were really questions: What is its density? What is its melting point? Will it oxidate? Some of the questions were useful to ask; some were not. If you had a mineral, asking its boiling point was meaningless, but stumbling upon the question of its fracture angle unlocked everything. Once we found the correct set of questions to ask, we gradually uncovered the chemical structure, and were eventually able to supply our professor with the substance's correct name. He, of course, knew all along what it was. The substance was itself the answer; our job was to find the right questions.

Toward the end of writing my memoir, I realized I was becoming disgustingly, though perhaps not surprisingly, self-involved. Bitter and jealous, I stalked my own list of personal grievances. In particular, I was jealous of a woman who had cervical cancer; I thought she got to have all the 'benefits' of a hard experience but didn't have to suffer any permanent visible scars. She was beautiful and had just fallen in love with a friend of mine. I felt ugly and had just broken up from a traumatic affair. Able to see I was turning into something I didn't want to be, I kept trying to 'get a new outlook'. Eventually, after realizing there was no way to think my way out of this depressing state, I decided on real-world action. I called up a hospice and volunteered to help dying patients write their own memoirs. It was an act of pure ego. I thought I would finally be able to view myself as that kind, loving person I so always wanted to be. As it turned out, most of the patients were too debilitated either to want or to be able to write, or even dictate, their stories. Most of the time I spent volunteering was spent sitting or standing next to a bed, offering what the hospice calls 'a ministry of presence'. I held on to their hands, I stroked their foreheads. Sometimes I rubbed their feet, which was difficult, because it is true: The body dies in increments. The feet often go first, and what I had to take in my hands was often scaly and flaccid. I always thought of Christ washing the feet of his apostles. For me, it was pure symbol. For the them, it was kindness, perhaps some small relief.

After several weeks on the in-patient ward, I noticed a curious thing. Many of the nurses, aides, and other volunteers were in the habit of bringing men they were interested in into the hospice to meet patients they were particularly fond of. Ostensibly this was so the boyfriend could see part of his girlfriend's life, but as soon as he left there'd be a great conspiratorial rush to the patient's bedside. 'So what do you think of him?' In the past the dying have always been assigned great mystical powers of truth-saying, and in the way my new lovelorn co-workers hung on to the patients' slow, painful words, words sometimes metered out a breathless syllable at a time, the same belief lived on. They'd lean over the patients, in a ward always overheated and overlit, asking their questions with the belief that there is a final bottom to a person, that we can hit upon and distinguish a person fully if only we throw the penny down the well far enough, and that it is only the dying who are unencumbered enough to tell us how.

When Jesus was on the cross, depending on which gospel you're reading, he says several different things. One of them is a question. 'My God, my God, why hast Thou forsaken me?' Except, he doesn't even really ask that – in the two gospels it's present in, it's presented first in another language: '*Eloi, Eloi, lama sabachthani*,' *Eloi* derived from Aramaic; or, '*Eli, Eli, lama sabachthani*', *Eli* derived from Hebrew. The 'original' is offered so we readers can fathom why those near him misunderstand and think he's calling for Elijah. There is more written on this one verse in the gospels than perhaps on any other. 'Is Jesus quoting the twenty-second Psalm?' the writing asks. 'Is it instructive: Is He questioning God so that we can see that it's acceptable to have moments of doubt?' It's when I read people writing about the Bible that I feel the most alien from religion, and also when I feel the most sorry for us all. Many interpreters have gone to great pains to prove that Jesus' question is answered; after all, it's followed in one gospel with 'Father, into Thy hand I commend my spirit.' Surely, that statement right there shows he was answered, doesn't it? And yet, in truth, Jesus' last living sound is neither question nor comment, but a cry, a loud cry (John 15:37). Even this 'cry' has been under intense scrutiny, some writers going so far as to change it to 'voice', and declaring it wasn't a wail, as anyone else being crucified might let out, but actually a cry of victory, as if it would be too much for them to know that Jesus' last words were wordless, a cry of deep sorrow and pain. The need to know, the need to have it all be allright, to all make sense.

What hasn't been written on very much, though, is that fact such a crucial moment in Christianity centers on a moment of translation. Other than the use of *Shibboleth* in the Old Testament, these last words of Jesus are the only moment of translation in the Bible, the only moment when alien words are included as part of the whole meaning. I view this as being about how sometimes we can't understand each other, and need someone to intercede for us. That the final truth doesn't exist in one parcel of words or the other, but in both, and more important, in the space between the words, in that brief moment after you read the foreign words, yet before they are explained.

Frank had been dying for two years, though they'd told him dozens of times that only months were left. Everyone on the ward had a chance to get to know him well. Near the end he was on four grams of morphine a day; four *milligrams* is more than most people could take. He was like a man underwater, all his responses slowed to almost a halt. Often, he'd fall asleep in mid-conversation, even mid-gesture, freezing in place, and you had to wait for him to wake up. My friend Phoebe, his nurse, brought him blue irises one day, and also her boyfriend. Frank held the unopened irises one at a time and flicked at them with his forefinger and thumb, ever so slowly, to make them open, a trick his mother had taught him, and she had insisted they must be flicked twice. They opened, coming to life one at a time, so slowly, so very slowly, yet quicker than it took Frank to finish his second flick.

After the boyfriend was sent out for coffee, Phoebe leaned over Frank's bed. I was holding on to his feet, hot from being under the blanket I'd just pulled back off them. 'Frank, what do you think?' Slowly, he told her, 'I don't want to give you bad news.' 'What, Frank, tell me. You didn't like him?' Frank held his arm up to look at his watch, and then actually fell asleep in that position, his arm held up in front of his face, his body wrapped up in a blue cotton blanket. Phoebe didn't get that he'd fallen asleep. 'Frank, you can tell me. Is it bad?' Then she realized and started to laugh. The recent graduate of an amateur acting class, she looked up at me; 'Frank is always turning my dialogues into monologues.' Then the boyfriend walked back in. He seemed a decent enough person to me, carrying a streaked brown cardboard carrier with three particularly bright Styrofoam cups. It had been raining all day and water dripped off the coat he hung on the door. He didn't say anything. The three of us sat there, waiting for Frank, waiting for him to wake up and turn Phoebe's monologue back into a dialogue, waiting for him there with his irises, holding our unnaturally white cups of coffee.

A BRIEF SKETCH OF MYSELF AT FOURTEEN

I WAS RIDING COCOA, and the last thing I remember is Lisa riding Eddie past me at a canter, something I'd specifically asked her not to do and for exactly this reason: The next thing I remember is Cocoa's hoof precisely in front of my face. I was on the ground, I knew that much; brown bubbles of water pressed out around Cocoa's thick, creased heel as her metal shoe sunk into the wet ground. I did not yet understand that my body was hanging, feet first, from the fence, and that only my head was on the ground. Turning my eyes and looking up, I followed the line of her leg from the heel up to her muddy elbows; I hadn't brushed her properly before saddling her. Her stomach, all wet from the puddles, was a revelation. I saw now how clearly round her underside was, how long, how elliptical, how perfect. The subtle, secret line of flesh drawn where one half of the body meets the other extended itself from her white, hairless belly button to the dark, soft mounds of her udder. The one back leg I could see was stretching and pointing up to the white, just-rained sky, like an arm pointing out an unusual plane or exotic bird passing by. All this quiet, even peaceful observation took place in a year's worth of seconds, in the few inches between myself and a broken skull. 'Hmmmm,' was all I could think to myself.

We all knew Cocoa bucked, and bucked like a pro when

given even the slightest chance. I rode her anyway. She was 'my' horse, at least for a few weeks. Technically, of course, she belonged to Mr Evans, who owned the hack barn I worked at along with half a dozen other kids, not for money but in exchange for free riding. Each of us, unable to afford our own horses and too ignorant to get real jobs at real stables, fell in love with different hack horses at Mr Evans's barn by turn.

Ray, who'd worked there the longest, got to pick which horse was 'his' when a new selection arrived, then Lori did, then Lisa – who already 'had' Eddie – and so on down the hierarchical line. I was at the bottom. The horses left for me to pick, or which any of us picked really, in the end broke our hearts not through any of their numerous faults, but the world's, because we had to watch them be worked half to death, their mouths pulled and their sides kicked by huge city louts out for a day of fun in the faux country, a few acres of woods surrounded by housing developments. The flat-roofed, plywood barn was falling apart, and housewives from the surrounding neighborhoods were always calling the Department of Health to complain about the rats. There were a lot of rats. They scrambled for cover anytime you entered an aisle, and more than once I had to pull a drowned one out of a water bucket. Most of the horses didn't live in the barn, however, but in three small corrals surrounding the barn. Anything green had been eaten long ago, and when they weren't working, the hack horses just stood there. Summer and winter were okay, but in spring and fall the mud was so deep that the continuous, gritty moisture gave them something called 'scratches,' and the hair fell off their chapped ankles in infected, painful-looking scabs.

Like all the horses at the stable, Cocoa had come from the auction, a weekly Wednesday-night affair filled with dog-food dealers, alcoholic cowboys, and almost-bankrupt barn owners. It wasn't a place for million-dollar racehorses, or even decent horses someone might want to own privately. It was a place to unload problem horses, soured horses that bucked, kicked, or bit, and crippled horses, horses that would never be sound. Yet still, week after week after week, we begged Mr Evans to let us go with him. We lived by tales of people who had good horses but were pressed for quick cash, and each week we kept waiting for such a bargain to be led into the small area in front of the auctioneer. And, of course, we always felt that even if we got a horse with a few problems, we could fix those problems, and we waited for those diamonds in the rough too, certain we'd be able to recognize them from across the dirt ring.

The auction ring and the makeshift stalls around it were set up under a huge array of outbuildings. In spring and fall the ground got so muddy wooden planks were laid lengthwise down the aisle so you could make your way through the puddles. In winter, this mud froze into a gray cast of footprints both horses and humans tripped over. In summer, it was all dust, and the water buckets held up with bailing twine were always empty.

None of this squalor mattered to me. I loved horses, and if this rough world was part of that love, then so be it. The auction was always crowded All those human voices rising and converging in the air over our heads, punctuated by the loud shrill whinnies horses make when they're in a strange place. You had to be careful standing next to a horse's head at the auction, because he could let out a bursting whinny right next to your eardrum if you weren't observant enough to see it coming. Most of the horses there were destined for 'the meat man', the dog-food dealer, but it was something other than their physical worth to humans that thrilled me when they whinnied. Each horse had its own way of letting you know it was about to call out, but usually it was ears that pitched exactly forward, a tail lifted up, a neck just starting to arch, a horizontal line of muscles just starting to show on their sides as they took a deep breath. When I saw those moves I took half a step back and watched the horse whinny, its eyes large, its mouth half open, its nostrils so wide you could see the deep purple inside. Something which had nothing to do with any of us humans, or with the various shapes of human sadness we forced those bedraggled, doomed horses to inhabit, shone at that moment.

Cocoa was so named because of her chocolate-colored coat. I rode her even though she bucked because, not yet burdened by any actual knowledge of the details of horse training, I imagined she bucked because she was unhappy. I would make her happy, and because I thought that to be happy must equal being loved, I would let her know I loved her. It seemed so simple. I brought her carrots, I brushed her, I put my small, thin arms around her neck. I confided in her, told her that I understood what it was to be unhappy, confessed that I would probably have bucked too.

It is always men who want to push forward certain theories about why adolescent girls love horses so much, want to explain it in terms of sex, or the desire to be near such power. What do they know? What do they know, with their early childhood fixations, with their small hard bodies that point them so easily and so early toward what they think they want? What do they know of sensuousness unbound by form, of desire so unfocused it doesn't yet have a name, and doesn't even want one, desire fulfilled only by the very act of desiring itself? I *loved* those horses.

Cocoa never stopped bucking. Mr Evans, fearing a lawsuit, put her back in the trailer a few Wednesdays later. I wasn't there when they took her away. I turned my attentions toward the next candidate: Boone, a mild-mannered Appaloosa I came to love more than life itself. Boone stayed at the stable for years, allowing me to love him, but I also understood he'd never amount to all that much in the equine world. Then, every once in awhile, a horse like Cocoa came along, a quality horse except for the fact there was something invisibly 'wrong' with her; spoiled goods. Horses like Cocoa broke my heart, not because of the thing 'wrong' with them, but because, despite every dedicated ounce in my body, I could not fix that wrong thing. I could not do it.

And though any place was better than being at home, the stable was not an easy place to spend time; my fingers swelled and turned so useless in the winter I couldn't undress myself afterward in the garage, where my mother made me go because I was so dirty. In the summer the hay stuck like needles to my drenched shirt, sticking me whenever I lifted my arms over my head or tried to lean back in a moment of rest. When I undressed at night, bits of chaff fell from my clothes like confetti. I was working the work of a grown man for no pay, was bullied by the older kids for my assorted physical and emotional shames, and my romantic heart cringed at the sight of each broken-down horse, but still, I did not know how to find, or even name, any other place to be.

Without understanding it, we were mistreating those horses. We didn't know it was wrong to feed horses cattle feed, which we did when short of cash because it was cheaper. We didn't understand why the hay was always moldy and yellow, despite the obvious fact we bought only the cheapest and stored it improperly. A vet only rarely stepped foot on the place, and only then because a horse was near death. We didn't have the money for everyday vet calls, so instead we were always treating raging infections with bottles of hydrogen peroxide, stitching up wounds with sewing needles and without local anesthetic while someone else 'twitched' the horse to keep it still, which involved wrapping a chain tightly around the soft tissue of the horse's upper lip. They'd twist their head and roll their eyes back and freeze into a trembling standstill, more afraid of the pain from the twitch than anything else we could do to them.

My adult self looks back on all this and sees something avoidably sad. My adult self sees how I willed myself to stay there despite the unhappiness, because as a child, and for too long as an adult, I could only gauge how much I loved something by how much it hurt it me. My adult self looks back on these days and thinks, What a shame; it didn't have to be this way.

What does she know? What does she know with her theories of co-dependence, of mental health, of how it 'should be'? What does she know with her adult forgetfulness of what children know about loneliness and love, about how we are *always* trying our best, despite what the adults tell us? Those horses were muddy and skinny and filled with worms, but when I ran my hands down the articulated bones of their legs, or rested my head against their barrel-chested sides, the secret luminous truth of how wretchedness and joy are inseparable brushed past me, and sometimes it was almost as if I'd heard its rustle; so many times – myself alone in the dirty tack room, or at night turning out all the lights and locking up, or walking across a field to find a thrown shoe – my young self suddenly stopping and turning her head, listening for something she hadn't quite heard, something already gone, if it had been there at all. I *loved* those horses.

The people who came out from the city to rent horses rarely got their money's worth. Though some horses, like Boone, were well-behaved, their goodness only made it harder for them: Hackers ran them into the ground. The hackers brought the horses back heaving, covered with sweat, foam dripping down from under the saddle, and would tell us what a great time they had. Since Boone was 'my' horse, almost weekly I had to watch this happen, had to go hide in the tack room and wait out my sadness.

But not all the horses were so naïve. The stables were at the bottom of a gently sloping hill, and the trail wound its way up around this hill. For the first quarter mile the hackers and their horses were in plain view and the horses, however grudgingly, plodded forward. But then the trail turned and became obscured by trees, and the horses understood the exact spot at which they could stop in their tracks and start eating leaves. Most people who came to our stable didn't have a clue about riding and all their yanking and kicking meant nothing to the horse. Soon they'd start calling for help. Secretly proud of the horses, we'd ignore the hackers' cries for help unless Mr Evans was around, in which case we'd take turns going up and 'rescuing' the riders. At least a few times on a busy day, people complained.

'These horses don't go!' they'd shout at Mr Evans.

'You just can't ride, that's the problem.'

'I can too ride. I took lessons at camp. These horses suck. They won't move.'

At this point, Mr Evans would turn and hope I was around, because I was particularly effective for this specific stunt.

'I bet that skinny little girl could make that horse go.'

'I want my money back!' the hackers complained, as if money could solve all this, allow them to wash their hands of this dissolution and walk away clean.

'If that skinny girl can't get this horse to go, I'll give you your money back.'

It's true, I was very skinny, and underdeveloped; I looked utterly powerless. Most of the time, my body was an embarrassment.

I stepped up to hold the horse while its rider clumsily climbed down, grunting and often almost pulling the saddle off with them. The horse knew the routine, and as I stepped up to him to take the reins, he'd eye me sideways and try to step away as the disgruntled hacker crossed his arms and watched.

Knowing exactly who I was, the newly rehabilitated horse began hopping in nervous circles while I put one foot in the stirrup. Mr Evans had to hold the bridle because otherwise the horse would take off at a full gallop during that vulnerable second after I'd jumped up but before I'd actually landed in the saddle. I wondered how the customers could not have caught on. Once up in the saddle, and without bothering to put my feet in the stirrups, all I had to do was point the animal beneath me in the right direction and off we'd go with a clattering of hooves, leaving everyone behind to stand on the rocky ground, the quick four-beat gait smooth as anything, the wind pressing my shirt against my body. I liked to glance down and see the hard, packed dirt of the trail slip beneath us, the galloping horse's leg reaching out as if to grab that ground and pull it toward us while the leaves of a few low branches touched the top of my hair.

This was the moment I dreamed of, always, before I had ever been on a horse, before I knew I wanted this moment but wanted it nonetheless, and it was this moment I would keep dreaming of all my adult life. Galloping up and away in a smooth commotion of silent, eternal thrill, the simultaneous flying embrace both from and of the world. It was this moment exactly, except, as I reached the top of the hill where I'd maybe spin the horse around a couple of times for effect, I began to remember that this moment was surrounded by other moments. I still wanted this moment of galloping exactly, but as I turned back toward the stable, I also knew that I wanted it someplace else, under different circumstances; this moment exactly, but in a different moment. If I had my own horse, if I could become rich and rescue Boone from this grassless place, or if I could become smart enough and good enough to rescue a horse like Cocoa, if I could transform her into something 'right', or if for some sudden and miraculous reason whatever horse I *was* on could suddenly *want* to be stretching forward like this, out into what seemed like an endless chance, *then* I could live in this syncopated, enraptured moment forever, with desire being nothing more complicated than the pure, honorable link between me and rest of the world.

For now, for effect, I held the reins lightly, and the small crowd I was galloping toward would began to step back in alarm just as I pulled up short in a breath of dust. Dropping the reins across the horse's neck, I'd nonchalantly throw my leg over the saddle and jump the long distance down, landing with a thud to make sure everyone watching understood that I did not give a shit about a single thing is this world.

'See,' Mr Evans would say, turning to the silenced, still irate customer.

WRITTEN IN FOUR VOICES FOR THE *HUNGRY MIND REVIEW* ISSUE ON REGIONAL WRITING

I'M SO GLAD WE got this taxi; it's so hard to get a taxi in the rain. Look, there's one of those *boxes* again. On like every other street corner, next to a squat blue *New York Times* coin vending machine, are those brightly colored plastic *things* – I don't know quite what to call them because they don't *vend*, they open up for free – with 'Gotham Writers' Workshop' written on the sides. They'll usually be next to a free *Village Voice* plastic-box-thing, and chances are good, just like with the *Times* and the *Voice*, the box will be empty. Sometimes some nice person will leave an empty soda can festering with flies in there, but I've never actually had the pleasure of beholding a *bona fide* course description in there. It's a total mystery. I mean, for as long as I've lived in New York, I've seen ads advertising these workshops, but I've never actually met a *real live* person who's attended or taught one. I don't even really know, come to think of it, exactly what the Gotham Writers' Workshop *is*, I mean really *is*. Are they, like, serious? Do *real* writers go there? Should *I* go there? I figure they must be making money because they're so around, but I don't have the time to research it right now because here I am, late for yet another reading. Tonight's reading is at KGB's, that smoky bar in the East Village with the red walls? I can't remember who's reading, but it must be someone I know because I wrote KGB, 7:00, down in my date book, see?

No, no, Grace Paley read *last* night, up at the 92nd Street Y. I just love Grace, don't you? She's so New York, mostly because she left it to go live in Vermont; how more successful New York Writer can you get? Maybe Brett Ellis will be at the reading tonight. We have this whole thing going where, like, we've never actually met but we know who each other is, so we, like, look at each other. Or at least I think he knows who I am. Maybe I'm just on an ego trip. Not that I care or anything.

Did I tell you I had dinner with Allan Gurganus the other night? He was in town for some book thing, I don't remember what. That's the thing I love about being here; everyone passes though sooner or later. Of course, I had to rearrange my meeting with Rick Moody – didn't you just *love* the movie of his book? – and I had to bump Sebastian's party to make the dinner, but that's okay, I can see them anytime. Sebastian's party? Oh, that was him celebrating yet *another* year on the *New York Times* Bestseller list. That dog. Oh, yeah, we go way back, gave our first readings of our books together long before they were even books.

I can't believe I have to go to *another* reading *tomorrow* night. At the Nuyorican, of all places. A friend who's in his forties and been writing for years, but who can't get an agent or publisher interested is reading there. I don't get that place, the Nuyorican. The Nuyorican? The Nuyorican is where a lot of Poetry Slams take place, and a lot of Spoken Word readings happen there. It's got a long 'indie' kind of history they'd be happy to tell you all about if you asked them. But that's the whole New York thing, isn't it; all these different sub-writer-culture-worlds? Spoken Word is *huge*, and yet I really don't know that much about it. Do I sound like an elitist ignoramus? So be it. I mean, there's just *no way* to keep track of all the different things going on around here. Am I supposed to try?

Or does one just pick one's niche and learn all you can about *that*? By the way, do you think I should change agents? Who's your agent?

I am *so* far behind in my work it's scary. Apart from the two books I have due, I have *three* magazine articles due like yesterday. I *hate* writing magazine articles, but they pay so much, how can you not? Most of my other writer friends have to have boring day jobs in order to support their writing habits, so I guess I should grateful. Complaining must be a hobby for me, because I seem to spend a lot of time engaging in it. Poor little me. Teaching doesn't really pay the bills, but at least it's steady income and it makes me sound semi-official. I mean, I get an office and mail addressed to *Professor*, har-har. All these major writing programs right here in the city – Columbia and New York University, as well as the New School and Brooklyn and Staten Island, and who knows where else. This city is *crawling* with writing students. At least it fills up the seats at the readings.

Do you really think they'll all become writers, these writing students? That's a scary thought, isn't it? Imagine a whole scary city filled with scary writers. Yikes. Did I tell you about this silly awards dinner I have to go to next week?

– Excuse me for interrupting, but I can't take it any more. Cab driving is only what I do when I'm not writing plays. All the way down Fifth Avenue you've been monologuing about the writing life in New York, yet you're acting like a character in a Robert Altman movie that's poking fun at the writing industry. You don't really mean to suggest that here in New York, *New York*, the world's intellectual hub, that the writing world has been reduced to endless readings and name droppings and the search for an agent, do you? Do you? Do you mean to take the objectively historical and make it merely personal? Just think of the history here; each and every block has been walked by writers, famous and unknown. Apart from all the writing *about* New York from Crane to James to Baldwin, there's the simple fact of all the writers who have lived here, have allowed the chaotic essence of New York to enter their sentences. The Beatniks in the village, Frank O'Hara and the other New York Schoolers, the Harlem Renaissance writers, good old Paul Auster over in Brooklyn. In the last two hundred years, right here on this soil, the very *idea* of writing – what it is and why it means – has been re-invented a thousand and one times, and, while it's true the modern dilemma has been to write the historical epic which is also modern and thus located in individual consciousness, all *you* can do is complain about how *young* all the editors are now and how pornographic Times Square has become since Disney moved in. Doesn't the post-modern dilemma of the broken yet unfixable narrative worry you at *all*?

– Jesus, you sound like you've been reading the Culture Section of the *Times* for too long, my cabbie friend. I may look to you now like just another squeegee man, trying to earn a buck as I wash your window with filthy water while you wait here at this traffic light, but I used to own a small independent book store in Midtown. Remember when Midtown was famous for having small independent bookstores? When you could go to a bookstore and find a small-press, out-of-print book and maybe stand behind Saul Bellow in line at the cash register? You think this young woman should be *grateful* to be a writer living in New York? Ha! My limousining friend, don't you understand that even as we speak you can hear the slow tick-tock of the petrification of the writing scene in New York? Why don't you take them for a 'tour' down the to the Cedar Tavern, or over to the White Horse so they can see the barstool where Dylan Thomas drank himself to death? Then you can pop over to some open-mike place where all the readers confuse the value of their political right to speak with the value of what it is they have to say. Don't you understand it's all about money, that multi-national corporations *own* not just the bookstores, but the printers and the distributors and the editors *and* the writers? And that even when we are permitted into thinking that writing as it is embodied here in New York is bold and edgy and radical, that this is really just another form of the commodification of dissent? The danger is not that we are *not allowed* to say anything truly radical, but that we think we *are* saying something radical.

– Move it along, you people; the mayor of this town has outlawed squeegee men and gypsy cabs, so I as an officer of the law must ask you to disperse. But before you go, I couldn't help overhearing your comments. Though I do this for a living, I actually have an M.F.A. in poetry, and though I see your argument Mr Squeegee Man and support aspects of it, it just so happens that I *do* think it is possible to both write as an individual independent of standardizing business concerns *and* to participate in the 'culture' of the New York writing scene without succumbing to its accompanying false and self-serving sentimental notions. The whole point is that simply by living in New York you have access to a large number of writers and cultural institutions, and there are also many and various outlets and venues in which your writing can be published and heard. Though to a non-New Yorker this may create the impression of a cohesive and even desirable 'community', the truth is that much of the writing scene in New York takes place in private conversations over cheap noodles in Chinatown, pints of beer on the Upper West Side, and e-mail conversations that privacy laws would allow us access to only in the event of a federal crime. Sure, there are tons of writers' groups and reading groups and all that, but there hasn't been a significant aesthetic manifesto out of New York as a locale for decades now. So don't worry about it so much; keep writing, pay your parking tickets and for God's sake put that dung away.

– Every time I try to have a conversation with anyone, *this* is what happens. I mean, how is anyone supposed to say anything *meaningful* in the middle of all these interruptions? Are we there yet? I don't think I have anything smaller than a twenty.

THE STORY SO FAR

THE FIRST TIME HE left a message, I knelt there on the carpet, staring intently at the answering machine. His flat voice asked me to call him, leaving only a name and number. Suspecting he was a bill collector – I was continuously in debt – I instructed myself to start screening calls. He phoned once more when I wasn't in, and left another message, a slightly more specific one that mentioned Tennessee. Two days later, he called again when I *was* in. I sat on the blue couch, perfectly still while his voice groped out blindly through the magnetic tape, afraid to move, as if I'd give myself away.

Provincetown was my home that winter, on the tip of Massachusetts' Cape Cod. I was writing a memoir that would eventually bring me a kind of low-volume success. My apartment, which I rented for only fifty dollars a month, was right on the water, offering itself up to any and all bad weather. To me, this was the best feature of the apartment: the wind howled so dramatically I had begun to speak back to it, while the whole building, a three-story house, swayed enough during a storm that I could see the water in my toilet bowl slowly sloshing back and forth. This was true of the water in the bathtub too, a place I spent copious amounts of time. I was heartbroken that winter and the steaming water I lowered myself into each night felt, to me, the only thing willing to hold me, that had any patience at all.

Despite the rest of the year's heartbreak, that Christmas was the best I'd ever experienced, primarily because I was putting into action a rule I'd discovered in graduate school: Be nowhere near your family on holidays. I roasted a turkey and invited everyone I knew. With my small apartment stuffed with friends who kept letting the toilet run and the indoor cat outside by mistake, I was happy. I was so happy and involved that when the phone rang, I picked it up without hesitation.

'Hello?'

'Is this Lucy Grealy?' the dreaded voice asked.

It was the bill collector. I was caught. In that split second, I thought how it was a dirty trick to trap someone on Christmas. I imagined him stealing my name from some application form.

'Who is this?' I asked.

In the next split second, I made a sudden delirious decision to get my life back in order. I would 'fess up, pay my bill, and then, as if bidden by this good deed, everything else that was good in the world would march right into my life.

'Are you the daughter of Desmond Delargy Grealy?'

The vision of the glorious new order in my life vanished. I had not heard the full, three-tiered name of my dead father said aloud in many years. I'd said it myself a few times, the answer to official questions under the fluorescent light of insurance company offices, but I had not heard it said by a stranger since his funeral, fifteen years before.

'Yes,' I told the man on the phone.

'And are you the sister of Sean Grealy, and of Nicholas Grealy, and Susan Grealy?'

'Susan? I don't have a sister named Susan. Who is this?'

'What is her name?'

'Who the hell is this?'

He told me. I don't remember his full name now, but his story was this: My brother, Sean Delargy Grealy, had a daughter named Margaret eighteen years earlier. Now this Margaret Grealy had hired him, a private detective, to find out everything he could about her long-absent father.

I faltered for a moment before speaking.

'I hope I'm not the first one to tell you this, but Sean died in a car accident, a little over a year ago. Or, actually, we found out a year ago: He'd already been dead for a year. That makes it two. Two years my brother's been dead.'

The irony had been that a year ago I'd been on a plane, flying back from three years of living in Europe, and on that flight I'd had the morbid fantasy of having to tell my mother about the death of Sean from AIDS. He was a long-term heroin user, and I figured this had to be his ultimate fate.

After my plane touched down at Kennedy, I went to visit my brother Nicholas, nine years older than I am. He buzzed me into his apartment but waved me into silence when I entered. He was on the phone, having an intense conversation. When he hung up he told me it had been a friend of Sean's, that she'd been trying to find Sean's family for the last year, to let us know.

The first thing we had to do was call my mother. I sat with the phone on the floor in Nick's narrow hall, smelling the smoke of his cigarettes embalmed into the plastic handset, and listened to my mother cry. She told me something then I'd never heard before: that of all the children, I was the one who resembled Sean the most. Not only in the way I spoke and thought, but even in the way I moved, the way I walked.

Growing up, Sean had been the great taboo subject in my family: Speaking of him upset my mother so much that we simply didn't. He'd been an angelic-looking child with a high IQ; a true golden boy, a favorite son. Then adolescent-onset schizophrenia was diagnosed, and then the drinking started, then the drugs, then he left us all for good to go live three thousand miles away.

When I was growing up, my mother would get into strange moods sometimes and talk about Sean. Before I knew how to recognize the signs of drinking, I thought it was the talking about Sean that put my mother in her mood. She'd take me to her room, sit me down on her bed, and explain how she had loved Sean the best, and how he had broken her heart, and how that was why she didn't, couldn't, love me. I sat there on the edge of her bed, hands between my knees, and nodded in empathy.

Despite all his problems, Sean, from what few clues we received, retained an almost uncanny charm. His friends loved him, remained loyal to him, no matter how often he harmed them. 'I can see that in you, too,' my mother told me on the phone, crying with the news of his death, 'Not the illness, but the charm, the way you have with people: You're just like Sean.'

Sean was thirteen years older than I. By the time he left home I was just learning how to remember. With only childhood pictures to guide me, and exactly one photograph of him when he was sixteen, I grew up with only a vague, ribbony idea of what Sean looked like. If he'd walked into the room and sat beside me, I would not have recognized him.

My family had known about Margaret's existence from her birth. We even had a tacky shopping-mall-style portrait of her, the fake trees in the background, the blue blanket she lay upon meant to represent a babbling brook. But Sean left her and her mother when Margaret was small, and we'd never heard from either of them again until now.

Though I had very little to tell this private detective, a few translucent memories, I agreed to speak to him on one condition: that he send me a copy of his final report.

* * *

For the ten years before I wrote my memoir, I'd been a poet, surviving on air and fellowships at colonies. I understood that becoming a poet was not financially rewarding. My almost accidental entry into the comparative riches of prose changed this: Suddenly, writing was not only the thing I did with my life, it was the way I paid my rent.

This changed me in subtle ways. Some of them were good. When I first sold the rights to the book, before I'd actually written it, a friend said when I told her the news, 'You better get a therapist.' But because we were in the middle of a heat wave, with the fans on *high* and the windows open, the traffic blaring below, I thought she said, 'You better get a hairpiece.' This made perfect sense. Of course I would need some sort of disguise. I was about to reveal so much.

The notion that writing a memoir would have any cathartic effect on *me*, of all people, was utterly silly. *My* writing was about the larger truths in the world, and had nothing to do with pop-psychology. Whenever anyone asked if I thought it would be a 'healing experience' to write my story, I felt vaguely insulted.

My reluctance toward anything that employed the verb *healing* had to do with an instinct that not only abhorred reductionism for aesthetic reasons, but which simply didn't believe healing was possible. Healing, as in 'made all better', as in 'gotten over', as in 'over'. Nothing was over, as far as I could tell.

While actively writing poetry, I'd developed an incredibly rigorous aesthetic, one which involved an almost religious honesty about specific moments, about rendering them as truly and clearly as possible. Having a preconceived idea about how a poem or an image was going to work was a sure way to produce a terrible poem or a forced image. One had to carefully watch how an image developed, learn to listen to it, be prepared to change one's expectations of it whenever it strained, like an adolescent, against the expectations of how it *should* behave.

Though I didn't have the language to describe it or even the desire to perceive it as such at the time, my student self's relationship to art was decidedly conservative. Narrative was my form of choice, though I often chose to mask it within the lyric; even when my images or topics were abstract, the way they flowed from one to another within a poem still described a fairly straightforward emotional journey. What I didn't yet understand was how complicated even the simplest narrative is (because at heart the act of narration is an act of faith in a world that can be followed), and also how complicated both my own life already was (though I wanted to believe it was simple) and how even more complicated it would yet become through my attempts – spiritually, emotionally, rationally – to understand this life.

Despite my deep-seated belief that there were certain things I would always suffer from (a low self-esteem; a belief I was ugly and unlovable), writing my memoir did help me close the door of some of these beliefs. How? Because my loyalty was to my writing (writing was how I learned to be loyal: I'd never considered it in regards to myself, or been given ample chance to apply it to anyone else), I was determined to produce not an account of my own victimhood, but a respectable piece of writing. And the only way to do this was to apply the same rigorous honesty to *my life* that I'd previously applied to abstract images and themes, to language. It was only when forced to place my own life under the microscope of my aesthetic that I realized two important things. One: that I'd undergone an extraordinarily difficult set of circumstances, something I'd previously never been willing to admit in my attempt to diminish and normalize those circumstances. And two: that I'd actually done not only well, but very well, considering those circumstances.

The process by which these revelations came about was simple on the surface: I had to go back and mentally, emotionally, re-inhabit my past. Simply, to remember what had happened. Oddly enough, when people later asked me about this remembering process, they asked in a tone that implied I had undertaken a great effort, that I had somehow painstakingly gone back and researched, rebuilt my story detail by painful detail.

In truth, it was not a building process, but a disassembling one. I did not have to go seek the details, I simply had to allow them to come to me. This involved placing myself in a state of mind which invited them back, and this, in turn, involved leaving all my judgments and preconceptions behind. Because what I found to be the greatest obstacle to remembering wasn't the effort itself, but the insidious nature of memory, how it confused itself with interpretation. How I *thought* about a particular event, how I felt it affected my life, interfered with my ability to actually remember the event itself clearly and purely. It was almost like reading a review of a movie before seeing it. My mind wanted to direct my attention to particular details and insist they were clearly meaningful, when, if fact, they might actually have seemed inconsequential at the time, or had a significance completely different from the one they would eventually accrue. A comment my mother might have made in passing, the way all our cats seemed to run away, the particular love of privacy and freedom I found alone in my musty, basement bedroom.

After my book came out and I dabbled a bit with therapy, I recognized the two processes as being essentially similar. An absolute allegiance to the truth was required, a letting go of how I had somehow come to think it was all *supposed* to be. Still, without doubt, and without my recognizing it, my greatest obstacle in therapy was the notion that I was somehow supposed to reconstruct a set of childhood memories that would explain, highlight, or at the very least underscore, the problems with intimacy and self-doubt that haunted me as an adult. Once I did this, told the right story in the right way, I felt, my problems would be exorcized like so many ghosts from an otherwise desirable house.

I thought it was still about the story, the narrative. Without my realizing it, popular culture stoked this belief; Hitchcock films such as *Marnie* and *Spellbound* insisted it was the simple act of remembering the forgotten which lead to curative wholeness, while even such innocuous television programs as *Gilligan's Island* and *The Bob Newhart Show* based whole scripts on the idea that single past events shaped entire lives, and that once again it was the act of conjuring up these buried events that brought about resolution and order, even if only comedic order, to one's life.

Despite a snobbism that ruled out the idea that I could be affected by popular culture's reductive interpretations of complex theories, I still believed Therapy, with a capital T, was all about the heroic act of remembering well enough, of finding the right story with just the right touches of pathos, cruelty, and indifference to explain the rather mundane emotional mess I'd found myself in.

My memoir was finally finished and published. People I hadn't heard from in years called me up to congratulate me. People I only dimly remembered, and some that I didn't remember at all, contacted me. One phone call came from a woman I had never met; she wanted to know if the Sean Grealy in my book was the one she had known in high school. After an exchange of verifying details, I told her yes, then told her the news of his death, which hadn't been part of the book. She broke down in tears. Awkwardly, over the long-distance phone line, I tried to console her.

Some weeks later an envelope appeared. It was late morning

when I fished it out of my mailbox, which meant it had actually arrived the day before. It was a large manila envelope. So much time had gone by, so many things had happened, that I'd forgotten. It was from Tennessee.

The private detective's report was eighteen pages long. Most of it covered my brother's life after he'd left home, when I was quite young. All these details about his life, things I'd never known, nor, I have to admit, had every really thought about. The names of his friends, his girlfriends, where he spent his time, the sad accumulation of details culminating in his falling out of the back of a pickup truck at one in the morning after the driver, a man named Peter, hit the base of a bridge as he was making a right-hand turn.

I sat there on my rug and read all of this: a stranger's life. And then, when I turned to the last page, I saw it was a photocopy of my brother's death certificate. They had his name right, and they had the time, place, and reason of death: massive head trauma. Also, he had lived 0 minutes after the injury. I didn't know there was space for that information on a death certificate, but it made sense that people might want to know such a thing. I hoped that the coroner – I'd never even used the word *coroner* before; it belonged to news reports and detective novels – was right about that zero. It made it easier.

But under every other heading on the death certificate-birthplace, age, occupation, father's name, mother's name, address, education, again categories I didn't even know they put on a death certificate – and typed in lower-case letters, was the same answer, over and over and over again: *unknown, unknown, unknown, unknown.* I lay down on the carpet and wept.

Then I realized it was time to go meet a friend. I cleaned myself up and solemnly went out the door, checking my mailbox on the way; the mailman was just leaving. In my box was a fat white envelope with a name and address I didn't recognize. I didn't know it as I took it out of the box, but it was from Sean's old high school friend, the one who had broken down on the telephone. She was sending me photographs she had taken twenty years ago, a yellowing set of pictures of Sean when he was sixteen or seventeen.

As I said, I'd only seen one picture of Sean when he was that age. What I haven't said yet is that I've only got one picture of myself from that age. I hated cameras, and successfully avoided them for the most part, except for one my older sister had taken of me when I was about sixteen myself. In it, I am sadly turning my head toward the camera, looking big-eyed and melancholy, but smart. I remember hating it at the time, but recently I'd seen it again and, maybe it was just youth, but I realized I'd unknowingly possessed a certain grace and beauty, despite the fact I'd thought myself obscenely ugly at the time. I'd been wrong, I understood, when that picture of myself resurfaced. I hadn't been ugly at all.

Walking down the street toward my friend, I opened this other envelope, still not knowing what it contained, and then stopped there on the sidewalk when I saw the top photograph. It was Sean, in a pose exactly like the one of myself. My mother was right; he looked just like me. The same forehead and cheekbones, the same eyes, the same hair, the same oval face, the same sad grace.

I walked into a bar in Greenwich Village. My friend was already there. I walked to the table she'd gotten for us, tossed the envelope filled with the photographs and the envelope with the report on to the wooden surface, and said, there: look at that and you will know exactly as much as I do about my brother's life.

As a poet, I'd lived a life in which romantic notions of truth and beauty and posthumous fame tempered the realities: a credit rating in the negative numbers, the knowledge I would never qualify for a mortgage or a credit card, the possibility of never living in one place longer than the average one-year term of an associate professorship. None of these things seemed too terrible. Perhaps it was simply that I was young. Perhaps I felt on the brink of something.

The truth is, I *was* on the brink of something. Publishing success. My memoir, coaxed out of me by an agent and an editor, gave me more money, and more opportunities to make money, than I had ever earned as a poet. The money from the book kept me afloat for three years just by itself, while the opportunities to write magazine articles, teach at well-endowed schools, and apply for larger, more prestigious grants all suddenly dropped themselves into my lap. Abruptly, I could afford an apartment in New York City. I could afford to fulfill a life-long dream: I threw out all of my clothes and bought an entirely new wardrobe. I traveled. I ate dinner in restaurants, and discovered I could distinguish a thirty-dollar bottle of wine from a four-dollar bottle of wine.

This wasn't a rags-to-riches story. I had not lived in poverty before, only a poorness as outlined for an educated white person, which essentially meant that previously I had to take the subway instead of cabs, owned not a single stock, and, as I said, was a failure on the abstract yet reified scale of credit rating. Always, I'd been aware of my privileges and my opportunities, an awareness which, no matter how many bill collectors I was avoiding, still highlighted the chasm separating my own relative poorness from the debilitating poverty experienced by fully two-thirds of the world's population.

Yet, once I tasted the comparative riches of my own society, once I learned I could make good money by writing, something changed in me. It's not something I'm proud of. I began assessing subjects in terms of whether or not I could sell them as ideas for a book or an article. Not to say that I turned into a money-grubbing little fool, but this much was true: I learned how to calculate things on a scale of worth that I'd never previously even considered.

So, when I told some friends and a few editors about receiving this private detective's report and the photographs in the mail, they all wanted me to write the story. Maybe just an article, maybe I could get a whole book out of it. I could travel out to California and retrace my brother's steps, reinhabit his life so that I could learn something about him. This could be connected to larger themes of what it means to have a family, what societal trends my alienation from my brother acted as paradigm for, what directions of healing might be gleaned from my own individual journey back to my brother. It sounded good. Everyone thought so.

Except for one problem. It was baloney.

Maybe, though, I could make it true. Maybe, by the very process of seeking out the facts, by putting myself through the experience of obtaining the narrative details of my brother's life, and then observing, reflecting upon, and writing about that experience, I could learn something true about my relationship to my brother. After all, I never suspected any 'healing' to come from the process of writing my memoir, so why was I balking now?

Before I began my memoir, I'd never been much good at prose, but I learned the craft of it while blundering my way through my book. Now, I was not only well paid to write prose, I actually taught it to people who looked at me expectantly, wanting not just the secret of writing, but the secret of success. Previously, I'd taught only poetry courses. There, not many people planned on getting huge advances for their books. And even if the majority of my poetry students didn't go on to live the life of a poet, I knew I had given them, or attempted to give them, something that transcended material notions of career: the knowledge of language, the intimacy of its powers and its beautiful, instructive failures.

But in my nonfiction classes, the most pressing problem was my students' belief that the story itself mattered above all else; the writing was only secondary, in their opinion. Not in mine. Most classes were dedicated to showing them this, trying to get them to believe that even eating a cheese sandwich could be an exciting, profound act if written well enough. But their beliefs persist, and whatever is on the bestseller list never helps: badly written accounts of interesting lives. My cheese sandwiches and I get left in the dust.

It was the Enlightenment which opened the doors for Freud, its idea that reason could ferret out the truth. In the centuries previous to the Enlightenment, much of medical science had believed that each body's disease was individual in origin, definition, and cure. There were as many diseases as there were bodies, and this belief helped medical practioners maintain their strong aversion to research and descriptive observation – why waste time developing a theory of how the body or one of its diseases worked when it obviously worked in an entirely different manner for each individual? It was only as late as the early eighteenth-century that doctors began to consider the value of studying and describing the various organs and their functions in any systemic or organized manner, and, by doing so, allowed for the new and surprising fact that diseases often ran fairly predictable paths through even a very large variety of patients.

Freud listened to his patients' personal stories and fit them into a universal template, the various Stages of Human Development. Each detail of a patient's life, no matter how particular and personal, pointed toward a larger abstract framework. Recognizing how their own sordid details fit into the subtleties of this larger truth was the only way, Freud believed, that his patients could begin to seek freedom from the pain associated with those details. And in the midst of all this scientific language, the actual heart of the process, the thing that was both diagnostic tool and therapeutic treatment? The telling of a story.

Perhaps the overwhelming desire for narratives nowadays is in part some strange leftover symptom from this. Today, in every nook and cranny of our culture, whether the bestseller list or the daytime talk show, there is an overwhelming desire for narrative – pure narrative, without the art of telling featured as a part of the story. The stories pour out of us. They never stop, because we never run out of stories.

But the possible larger truths our particular details might signify seem less easy to discern. What do all these stories *mean?* Before the Enlightenment, religion gave us the back-frame for our stories, which always underscored either our virtues or our sins. The Enlightenment gave us the idea of human development, which hinted, though Freud never did intend this, that everything was fixable. Now, either there is no larger truth, or we can't get to it. Either the moral majority is right, and our world is in moral decay because of the lack of 'values', or maybe money really is the root of all evil and has stripped us of the ability to say the truest thing. Or perhaps we have forgotten about, or have not yet been able to articulate, the newest version of what art means to us in this post-Enlightenment, post-religious time, and that is why we can't find the story that finally says it for the last time, or, maybe, it's always been this hard.

Going from being a writer of poetry to a writer of prose changed, in essence, my going from attempting to convey small moments of being which held within them the suggestion of larger moments of understanding, to attempting to convey understanding that resulted from the parceling out of relevant information at particular intervals. On top of this add my realization that I could actually make money doing this. I had not necessarily had all this in mind *while* I was writing my memoir, but subsequent to its publication, I could feel the way I moved about in the world, the way I perceived it, had changed.

My problems in therapy persisted. I often wondered what the hell I was doing there. I felt a strange pressure to be confessing things while in that room, or at the very least remembering in a heroic, tearful manner.

'I can *see* how the dynamics of my relationship with my mother get repeated in my relationships now, but I just don't get how that is supposed to change anything,' I complained to my therapist.

'Why is it supposed to change anything?' she asked back, in her typical therapist speak. I was always accusing her of therapist speak.

'Well, so then, what is the point of retelling the story? I mean, I just can't buy the idea that I'll stop feeling so lonely and unloved by recognizing that someone in my past allowed me to feel that way. I mean, I *feel* lonely because I *am* lonely.'

I was always thinking that therapy was trying to sell me some sham notion that my negative emotions were containable and controllable; that I was not in a relationship because I somehow engineered it that way, or that I secretly didn't want to be in a relationship. Why couldn't my therapist understand that I was not in a relationship because I was deeply flawed and no one wanted me? Why did she have to be so hardheaded about it? I sincerely thought that she thought that if only I could get the narrative of my early childhood straight, I'd recognize my barriers, walk out into the street, and find true love in the first single, appropriate man I met (as opposed to the unavailable, inappropriate men I was always pining for). Hogwash, I told her.

'Hogwash? What's hogwash?' she asked.

'That it's my *subconscious* that doesn't want me to have a relationship. I mean, really.'

'Is that what I said?'
'Isn't it?' I asked, tentatively.

When the story, or the facts as I had them, of my brother surfaced, and then the possibility of writing that story, for good money, followed, it was yet again my own aesthetics that forced my hand. All of the seductions to uncover the 'truth' of my brother's life were there, but I could not follow those seductions. Because another true part of *this* story, the one I am telling you now, is that I have already told a story, and another true part of *that* story, the one I told in my memoir, is that it doesn't even tell the secret, saddest story of my life, and in the artificial but useful hierarchy of the sadness of things, Sean's story holds a distant fourth.

Or perhaps I am kidding myself. Perhaps the simple, precise, and thus elegant trauma of my mother telling me she did not love me because I both was and was not my brother is the genesis of all my troubles. Evidence for this: the very first poem I wrote that worked, that 'clicked', when I was a freshman in college, was a poem called 'My Brother'. In the poem, I say not one true thing. None of the poem's particular details of searching for a lost brother is true. I made them up. But the larger desire that drives the poem, the desire to find something, someone, anything that will tell us we have found our home, is as true as it gets.

I do not know how to fit into this story the point at which therapy actually began to help. Sentences flow in a necessarily linear manner, and whatever self-understanding I've gained through therapy came about in a circular, roundabout manner that would bore the pants off of any reader if I tried to write about it. What is boorish and clichéd on paper can be profound and life changing in reality. Luckily, however, I have been offered by life one particular metaphor that contains within it the possibility for fathoming, all at once, my relationship with therapy, with my brother, and with my writing, and might possibly explain why I will not write, put into boorish and clichéd language, the plot of my brother's life. It is not a story about a single instance, but a repetitive one, a story that happens over and over, almost always the same in basic plot.

I always knew I had a brother out there, somewhere, and that he was probably, in some way, suffering. I knew he was mentally ill, I knew he was a drug addict, I knew he was sometimes homeless. But because I didn't know any of the facts of his story, the form of my acknowledging Sean's existence could happen not in any linear way, and so instead came, and still come to me in small moments of interchange that always offer the experience of deep understanding. I'd like to call these moments Poetic, but that labeling, because of all the attached meaning to the word, would suggest something sickly sweet, a made-for-TV act of healing. I'd like to call these moments Symbolic, but that suggests a culmination of meaning and experience which is transformative, and I balk at that notion because it, too, suggests some kind of resolution. Simply by writing about these moments I am, in form, forcing them into a Narrative, but no, that isn't it either. Sometimes the form of a thing *is* the thing, and sometimes it's only its shadow. I don't know how to tell you about these moments except to tell you about them.

They happen on the street, usually in doorways. It's actually a bit clichéd. Though it is not hard to give money to the sad, fallen-on-hard-times-looking homeless in New York, I know people find it more difficult to give to the obviously drunk and threateningly erratic. Though it resolves nothing, and perhaps means nothing, I have never had that problem. There is no larger narrative intruding, warning me for my own personal safety, or suggesting that I am perpetuating this person's problems, or this society's problems, by accommodating their sordid needs when, for a single moment, I hand that person on the street a stray, pitiful dollar, and that person, whom I will *never* meet again, takes it.

THE RIGHT LANGUAGE

THE LIBERAL LEFT IS accused unceasingly of not being able to communicate its ideas effectively. The liberals and the Left are being told, mostly by the Right and by the media, that their idea supply is bankrupt and that they just don't have anything more to say to the American people. This has been going on for some time, but possible reasons for this deficit of 'ideas' were underscored for me recently while reading a book called '*The Death of Common Sense* by Philip K. Howard. It is not exactly what Howard has to say, but how he says it and how it has been received by the Right that emerged as important to me. To Howard's surprise and exasperation, *The Death of Common Sense*, the politics of which drift between center and left of center, has been taken up, embraced even, by the political Right. How did such a misunderstanding happen? The answer is that Howard chose to speak his ideas in the Right's rhetoric, which, primarily, is the language of the anecdotal. And the political Right, in their own turn, borrowed this language from the religious Right.

There has always been a connection between religious fundamentalists and the political Right, but most of the comparisons focus on content, primarily on so-called Family Values issues such as abortion, single parenthood, and welfare. What has been paid less attention to are the similarities of how rhetoric is used by the two groups, and how this rhetoric distinguishes itself in its ability to silence the Left, not merely by not letting the Left get as captivating a word in edgewise, but by literally robbing them of the modes in which to successfully convey meaningful ideas.

It is important to note that while there are many political right-wing thinkers who are not ardent religious fundamentalists, there are few ardent religious fundamentalists who are not politically right-wing. Why should styles of thinking in religion inclusively allow thinking identified as political, while political thinking exclusively chooses only particular aspects of religious thinking to be openly associated with its own? The first part of this is easy to answer, especially if one compares what religious thinking does *not* have to fear with what political thinking *does* have to fear. Because religious thinking's starting point is one of universality, which is apparent in its relentless use of tautology, religious thinking has no fear of being subsumed by any political thought which enters into its rhetoric; because God has the last word, all things can finally only refer to that last word and thus either remain or become religious.

Political thinking, on the other hand, though it wishes desperately to appear universal, is also aware that it coexists with other systems of thinking. It carefully chooses those parts of religious thinking which pass on the veneer of universality while also carefully keeping a chain on the door to many other possible ways of thinking, and for good reason; most modes of religious thinking are adept at re-identifying a political thought so that a political idea suddenly finds itself serving the means and ends of the religious.

Religion is full of the anecdote; parable is one of its forms. Parables are short tales that mean something first by simply being a description of an event – a son who's gone astray comes home to a welcoming father. This first meaning is immutable insofar as there is little connotation to the description. But when the event is analyzed, a second level of meaning appears: God loves those who lose faith and then loves them all the more when they return again to faith. This second meaning is the end result of a specific process of analytical thought and is only one of the many meanings possible as the result of any number of ways to analyze the description of the event. However, to have that specific meaning reappear each time someone evokes that parable, the process of thought that produced it can neither be left to chance nor counted upon to surface of its own accord in each individual who reads the description of the event. To ensure the survival of the specific meaning, the specific process that leads to a specific meaning must be taught to individuals while other processes are strongly discouraged or even, ideally, eradicated. Survival of the idea most willing to kill other ideas, in other words.

Religious rhetoric relies on the use of parable not because it is the second meaning of the parable that is so important, but because the process by which that second meaning is arrived at is itself crucial. Because process is fluid and by definition possible of all kinds of mutations and swervings, it is extremely difficult to keep a firm hand on. Only solid things are easily controlled and thus ideal control of process can only come about from the reification of process, which is where the parable itself steps in. As a description of events it is immutable. In contrast, its second meaning, when there are any number of analytic processes available, remains open and various, but only so long as the processes by which the second meaning is arrived at remain visible and unobscured. To obscure the process is a very successful mechanism for controlling the process, and it's possible, by controlling the process carefully, to actually align the second specific meaning with the first immutable meaning so successfully that the second meaning itself takes on the quality of being immutable.

The political right-wing borrows this powerful reification of process all the time through the use of immutable anecdotes made indistinguishable from their second meaning. It is immutable that many people receive money from entitlement programs. That the government is failing to act intelligently and responsibly because many people receive money from entitlement programs is a second meaning arrived at through a particular, not universal, system of reasoning. Many right-wing politicians revel in constantly telling anecdotes about specific individuals who abuse the system. By constantly re-telling specific anecdotes, larger details of an event (larger in the sense they are available to more systems of interpretation) become obscured simply because there isn't space for them in which to be heard.

The words *tax* and *spend* are descriptions of two different types of activities. A possible second meaning is that liberals are wasteful, selfish, and foolish. Recently, through the use of rhetoric, anecdotes and sloganism in particular, this possible second meaning has been so successfully made to appear immutable that any questioning of taxing and spending as connoting anything other than 'wrong' has become almost impossible. Once this happened, discussion could then be limited, even by non-Right politicians, only to how taxing and spending can be curtailed; since no alternative second meanings are recognized, there can be no alternative routes of action. Disagreeing is simply no longer an option.

Alternative routes of action, therefore, can only be meaningfully discussed outside the realm of the specific logic created by such rhetoric. Fortunately, this is attempted continuously by people. Unfortunately, by definition, the process of linear, progressive, and reflective thinking must remain visible, otherwise assertions become confused with arguments, arguments confused with meaning, and meaning comes into danger of becoming falsely aligned with the immutable.

Still more unfortunately, the very word *visible*, usually an abstract notion when applied to language and thought, becomes an eerily tangible necessity. People need to 'see', that is, to take in all at once, a concept in order for it to become integrated into how they feel emotionally about something, and, for most people, it is necessary to have an emotional relationship to something as abstract as an idea before they will act on that idea. Applying a process to the seen thing delays that integration, so it can be infinitely more satisfying on an emotional level (especially emotions with which one is already well-acquainted) to simply keep 'seeing' things and apply no process at all.

Art steps in exactly here. It permits for things to happen all at once, as it were: You look at the painting, you watch the movie, you read the book. While you are taking it in, seeing it, there is little need to apply process; though, if you are so inclined, there is ample opportunity after the seeing. If what you see is purely satisfying, which is to say you are sated, content, then there is no need to apply process. If what you see evokes emotions neither normally associated with nor fully accountable to what one has seen, then only by applying process will something be understood and only then will any satisfaction be possible.

In the world of the purely intellectual, the desire to apply process is assumed. Thinking starts with the unknown and is used as an actual guideline; once something becomes clear through one process, it is time to apply the next process, a process that will in turn incorporate aspects of what has most recently become known. In the world of propaganda, the most suggestively insidious type of rhetoric, it is the already-known that is started with; next, all unknown things are rigorously subjected to an already specified process so that the unknown is transformed into becoming part of the already-known. In the world of art, the desirability of the unknown, if only as the provoker of thought, is assumed, but the already-known is also given value and its power to satisfy never underestimated.

A popular culture example of this is Charlie Chaplin, who in many of his movies presents the story of a man completely thwarted by all of his attempts to acquire food. Hunger is an already-known, but it is also by itself valueless: Only when it prompts you to seek food does it have value. If your actions are thwarted, then the thing hunger represents, starvation, becomes a serious threat to your survival. Chaplin is so provoked by his hunger that usually he cannot see beyond the hunger itself to its true source, which is ultimately whatever system is in place that repeatedly allows the hunger to go unsatisfied. Instead, he gets caught up with the details of it: the oven that will not work, the chicken that will not die, the baker who will not turn his back so that Chaplin can steal a loaf. For the viewer, it is a first meaning that Chaplin is hungry, and the first meaning solution is to acquire food. But free access to food is only a basic description of a need and, in this context, immutable. And it is only because we are the viewer, not immediately hungry but possessing a firsthand knowledge of what it is like to be hungry, that we have the leisure and the process to apply to Chaplin's problem and so come up with some possible second-meaning solutions. Chaplin, not surprisingly, was much beloved by the Left in this and other countries, and was seen as a serious enough threat in this country to be repeatedly denied the right to immigrate here.

Howard's book works, for the most part, on the level of the immutable. He describes specific events that portray individuals and organizations unable to get or do what they wish. Few people are drastically hungry in the book, but many wish to feed and house those who are. Specifically and also typically, one story chronicled is of a city church group that wishes to buy a building from the city and renovate it into a homeless shelter. The bureaucracy the group encounters that continuously thwarts the common sense that would allow this to happen would be humorous if it wasn't so exasperating to witness. Similarly, how an environmental law turns into an absurd farce when acted out strictly 'by the book' almost revels in the ridicule it opens the law up to. Howard relates continuously to the individual, showing how personal desire for and effort toward solving basic problems are discouraged in the present system, a system that devalues the individual.

But what makes this book open to the misguided endorsement of the Right is the Right's own appropriation, through their own anecdotes, the already-knowns Howard works with in his book, these being frustration, anger, and a sense of powerlessness. Within the logic of both the Right's and Howard's anecdotes, what comes through is about the lack of free access to the law, law that has grown exponentially in size over the last few decades. Within these anecdotes of recorded actions and verifiable facts, however, is a factor that is the undeniable product of second-level meaning: the law. Law is most powerful and most dangerous when it just is: no process of interpretation allowed. If the prohibition on interpretation is strong enough, or in place long enough so that people forget how to apply process, then the law successfully appears natural and immutable, even if only in that people feel powerless to change it. For the right-wing, who openly equate too much law with too big a government, the anecdote is an invaluable form. Within it it is easy to portray the law as immutable while at the same time, by showing individual difficulties with the law as exasperating, to convey the conclusion that regulatory law in the form of big government must be done away with as a solution that is itself immutable and unchallengeable.

Howard's anecdotes, however, are not meant to obscure the process either of the law or of how we interpret law, but to highlight these very things. Their agenda is not to make law appear equal to big government or to make either immutable. Instead, they embody the very opposite: Law itself is not immutable and closed to discussion and dealt with only in either/or extremist terminology; rather, it is the process of law, interacting with the law, which is immutable. The term *law* is merely a useful word for that process, more verb than noun. Knowing this, Howard's anecdotes become in actuality counter to what the Right wants them to stand for; these anecdotes are invitations for more, if different, applications of process, not fewer, and what is most difficult and most hopeful about this prospect is that part of this process is to be found not within the strict, already familiar confines of the legal system itself, but within that very human process known as thinking for oneself.

THE PRESENT TENSE

NOT THAT LONG AGO I went to visit my friends Eli and Danella in upstate New York. Eli and Danella have this life I'm completely envious of; they rent a nice little farmhouse situated on a gorgeous hill and live a secluded, arty life half the week, and the other half of the week they entertain friends. Because they both lead worldly, interesting lives, the people who visit them are worldly and interesting also. On any given weekend you can share the bathroom at Eli and Danella's with raving Romanian intellectuals, German astrophysicists, famous New York ballerinas, Italian magazine editors, as well as any number of writers and artists of varying fame and desperation. But the last weekend I was there I also shared the house with Tess, a black Labrador-ish bitch of uncertain ancestry. I particularly enjoyed sharing the weekend with Tess because, well, because Tess *liked* me. It didn't happen right away, it took some doing, and there were times when it looked like Tess would forever treat me just like any other stranger, with a kind of active disinterest, just like Big City dwellers learn to treat panhandlers. But I have to admit that I worked at gaining Tess's favor that weekend. To be well liked by a dog seems tantamount to some great ethical triumph. Dogs, we culturally assume, have some passport to our inner selves, and their 'like' of us is a justification of a self-image as an essentially good person.

Particularly interesting that weekend was watching how the other guests reacted to Tess. We were all of us silently courting her, trying to get her to linger by our chairs a tad longer than she lingered at others, trying to seduce her head into *our* laps as we sat by the fireplace. It was an unstated, not particularly vehement contest: Who would Tess like the best? And almost like cats who pretend nothing is wrong when they make an embarrassing mistake, it was curious to watch how each of us pretended it didn't bother us when Tess walked right by us when we called her, or that we weren't feeling just a little bit forlorn when we threw her the ball and she retrieved it with great glee, but returned it to someone else.

It was the Ball Game which was the great, all-telling paradigm when it came to each of our interactions with Tess. The Ball Game was Tess's hands-down favorite activity. Both Amy and Robert reported she could play it for hours. And perhaps *play* is the wrong verb, because Tess could undertake the Ball Game with a focused tenacity few of the humans in the room possessed. When you had the ball in your hand, Tess would crouch down in front of you, staring intently at the contents of your hands, willing you to perform. When the ball was finally thrown there was a great fumbling joy and a determination to retrieve it at all costs, and if it happened to land someplace where she couldn't reach it, Tess would stare and bark at its final resting place as if she could call forth the ball through sheer resolution. The yards she trotted back to you once she had it in her mouth spanned a happy calm, an almost post-coital contentedness.

But seeing if Tess would return the ball to you and not someone else was only the first hurdle. If you were lucky enough to be chosen, then there arose the problem of getting the ball back from Tess. Because for all of Tess's love of chasing the ball and her at times annoying imploring of you to play the Ball Game, once she had it, Tess didn't actually want to give you the ball. Her mouth full, she barked and whined and scratched at your feet, but she also resolutely refused to drop the ball. This could lead to a side game of tug-of-war, but because it was a ball at stake and not a length of rope, this wasn't particularly convenient from the human side of things. From the human perspective there seemed to be a great paradox brewing inside Tess: She wanted to play the Ball Game, and yet she didn't. It reminded me of a friend's two-year-old who screamed for a particular toy as if it were the Grail itself, yet threw it to the floor the minute you handed it to him.

Each of my fellow guests dealt with this paradox in a different way. One woman was immediately intimidated by the situation. She didn't want to put her hands anywhere near the dog's mouth and chose to simply give up, relying on Amy and Robert to distract Tess away from her. One of the men resolutely tried to get the ball back from Tess, through both physical and verbal cajoling. His failure seemed a great burden to him, and I noticed he surreptitiously spent the rest of the weekend trying to entice Tess's favor with bits of food.

I've spent a lot of time around animals, and when I played the Ball Game with Tess, I had a lot of ego and self-definition involved. Luckily for my ego, I was the only guest to successfully retrieve the saliva-soggy ball. Most people already know the Ball Game is not really a game, not purely in the sense that we humans use the word *game*. The Ball Game is an intricate yet subtle power struggle, a definition of who was alpha, and the only way to get Tess to give me the ball regularly and on command was to win the ball quickly and forcefully the absolute first time I played with her. I was harsh with Tess, demanding the ball in a stern, Dickensian-orphan-hater voice, and I know some of the other guests interpreted my behavior to her as cruel. But I did get the ball, and everyone was impressed. It was a yellow-greenish tennis ball, and when I held it aloft it spoke two languages: the first was to Tess, and the language was about a strict and highly regimented social order; the second was to my fellow humans, to whom the ball represented the fruits of a murky, mysterious 'knowing' on my part, the grammar of a secret animal language. The primary reason the other humans couldn't get the ball from Tess is that they viewed the imposition of a strict and regimented social order as deplorable cruelty, and so instead tried democratically to get the ball. I myself am a leftist from way back, but I do know this: Democratic language doesn't work with dogs; you have to be a lot more Republican about it.

Although there are a thousand and one different arguments about what exactly are the similarities and differences between animals and humans, the most useful distinction has to do with language. Language is primary to our experience as *humans*. All our desires, all our sins, all our arts, are rooted in our animals parts, but these enter human culture only when we pour in language and attempt to communicate the resultant mix to each other, and to ourselves. The single most important feature of human language is that it's abstract; you and I can talk about a ball even when there isn't a ball within a thousand miles of us, because we have a sound completely unrelated to the physical essence of a ball which can evoke it for us. Maybe you could say the word *ball* to Tess and she'd get excited and start crouching and looking for it, but my guess is that it's the *way* you say *ball*, the physical gestures and voice you use, that she's reacting to, that makes her believe a ball is physically imminent. And even if you could say the word *ball* to her with a still body and a completely monotone voice and she *could* recognize it, let's face it: you're not going to proceed to have an intricate, enlightening conversation about the finer aspects of the Ball Game with her. The Ball Game is pretty much the Ball

Game. It doesn't happen in abstract language; it happens on the plane of physical interaction, and for this reason is incapable of turning into something *other* than the Ball Game. In opposition, you and I could start out talking about the Ball Game, and then start talking about the Dodgers, then about Brooklyn versus Los Angeles, then about earthquakes, then about presidential visits to disaster sites, and then maybe finish up talking about the latest bill introduced before Congress. It's not so much the complexity of each of these individual topics that's important here, but the fluid fact that they can appear because of a linguistic link to what has preceded; we don't need a regulation baseball to break the window beside us in order to change the topic from the Ball Game to the Dodgers. Abstraction is crucial to the human sense of change and creation within a short span of time, and is, inherently, unfettered by the concrete, physical world. This is not to say that human language is 'truer' than what we might conceive animal language to be; anyone who's witnessed a pained look on a face, or heard a muffled cry, knows that physical language is a far more effective medium of conveyance than hollow sounds floating about in the air, or black scratches arranged on a white page.

This is probably the thing that strikes me most about communicating with animals. Physical interaction takes the place of talking. This is particularly evident in another of Tess's favorite games: Chase. To play Chase and have Tess delight in it, you have to forget about any possible goals; you simply crouch down a little and take a step toward her. She sees you, runs a few steps, then stops to look at you. You look at her, crouch again, then take some more steps toward her. It's that simple. Some people in the house thought it was about catching her, but that belief only led to frustration on their part, with Tess continuously getting unhappily stuck behind the couch. 'To be caught' is an abstract term because it takes place in a possible future. To enjoy Chase, you have to see it as taking place entirely in the now, and entirely in a language whose grammar is constructed of concrete movement and gesture.

This is not the way we interact with other humans most of the time. Because we have complicated, abstract things to communicate, and complicated, abstract ways of expressing these things, we're often not dealing with one another in the 'now' moment. We say things to one another with notions of how they *might* be received in the future, even if that future is only a second away, and as soon as we finish saying them, we are anticipating how we ourselves might react to something that *might* be said in the next second. The ability to linguistically leave time behind like this is crucial to the development of human science and culture; it's what we *are*. Yet, because of this way of communicating, we are often projecting on to each other not true representations of ourselves, but images and ideas of who and how we are *supposed* to be, who we *should* be, leaving behind who we actually might be.

Because we communicate with animals without abstract language, we feel freer and more able to experience truer senses of ourselves, our 'in the moment' self, with them. I think this is why some people feel safer in the company of animals, why animals are often capable of arousing deeply sympathetic emotions in us whereas our fellow humans fail to touch us quite so immediately and deeply. One-on-one, animals evoke true and profound parts of us; they seem to point to something deep within us. But this experience is fully open to us only when we play with them, when we actually undertake to communicate in ways that are experienceable by the animals. Because we can't truly know the soul of a dog, once we stop playing with that dog, everything becomes projection. Once the concrete interaction ends, the segue into abstract propositions is tempting and easy. To see the emotional fraudulence this can lead to, the sentimental havoc this might wreak, you only have to walk into a greeting card store, or sit down in a Disney movie. In these places, where animals routinely have the gift of human language, animals are no longer beings to be interacted with but spectacles to be watched – maudlin, oversweetened versions of ourselves, easily open to the uses of advertising. They are not only no longer real, they are unreal in the most insidious form of the unreal, by which I mean propaganda; Disney and Hallmark *et al.* allow and even encourage us to take a complicated personal encounter with an animal and reduce that encounter so that the animal becomes merely a projection of what we seem to think is our cuter self. The prospect of an actual encounter with the so-called other is excluded, and it's almost a relief; the cute is a lot easier to deal with and asks nothing of us. Even while on one plane animals offer us piercing insights into ourselves, on an alarmingly nearby plane our use of them also offers an easy path of halcyon simplicities, simplicities typified by the prevalence of the cute, of the idea of how we would like things to be winning out over the way things actually are. It's a process not dissimilar from the process that allows us to confuse political slogans with actual observations, or to think that whatever guilt or pain we may feel about the latest victims of the latest man-made disaster is by itself enough, that once we feel the appropriately dire emotion we can put the actual situation out of mind, or at least out of the realm of action. How much easier to do that, to allow a kind of symbolic emotional shorthand to prevail, than to do the grueling work required in making each interaction, whether with an animal, a person or a situation, remain real.

One of the things I love about visiting Eli and Danella is the dinner table. It's long and sits on an enclosed porch overlooking a long meadow. Danella's excellence as a chef is matched only by Eli's ability to produce endless amounts of wine, and dinner can go on for hours. The weekend I was there with Tess was a tense weekend for a lot of the guests; it seemed like almost everyone was waiting to hear about a job he or she was up for, a story an editor was holding on to, a visa crucial for some important travel plans. The conversation was giddy and fueled by our various anxieties; it was like we had to keep topping each other, each comment had to be smarter, funnier, more insightful than the last comment. It was evocative, intricate conversation, but it was also tiring at times; it took on the air of a competition. After we were done eating and just as the talk was reaching an even higher pitch, Tess began roaming around the table, briefly placing her head in each of our laps. She went from person to person, down the line looking for food, and each of us momentarily paused in chaotic mid-conversation to look down and stroke her head. It was a moment of comfort, a split second away from the talking. In the candlelight and with the dark meadow behind us, for a long few moments each of us was visited by Tess, making her rounds, and each of us by turn looked down and held her black, unpronounceably soft ears in our hands before looking back up and saying something else.

TWIN WORLD

PEOPLE ARE ALWAYS SURPRISED that I have a twin. 'Really?' they ask, almost suspiciously, 'You never told me that before.' They eye me as if I have just accidently slipped and revealed some clandestine past, unconciously displayed for them at last the tip of the mysterious iceberg heretofore known as me. 'Aha,' they actually say, and I can see them mentally rubbing their hands together, certain they are about to get to the bottom of my essential nature, that they have uncovered the missing clue.

And why not? The word *twin* all by itself is so inviting. The very sound of it inspires people. That single syllable conjures up a vast, complicated, twisting history. Spanning out from ancient mythologies trying to account for the world's duplicitous nature to current science trying to locate that murky line between what we are born to be and what we learn to be, the twin fascinates endlessly. The begetting of Romulus and Remus was the begetting of Western civilization. Nazi experiments on twins seem *extra* morbid. Diane Arbus's photograph of two little girls so obviously alike yet so blatantly different seems the natural choice for the cover of her posthumously published, ambiguous work. Many a good and a bad movie alike has resorted to the tried-and-true Evil Twin plot twist in order to get things moving . . . the list is endless because the idea of twins is endlessly compelling to people. People who aren't twins, anyway.

'I've always wanted a twin.' I hear that about half the time; the other half is more considered, less sure: 'I've always wondered what it would be like to have a twin.' In philosophy, Twin World Thought Experiments rely upon such imaginings. By considering that a second world exists with exactly all of the same phenomenal characteristics as this save for one prespecified characteristic, which is either altered or left out of the twin world, we might be able to learn something of how *this* world is formed, how things need one another, or don't, in order to exist.

If they had a twin, people generally seem to assume, they would understand something better about themselves. They would have a flesh-and-blood mirror to look into and see themselves. They would never be lonely. They would know what Plato was talking about when he spoke of 'the missing half'. They would finally get to the bottom of all this *nature versus nurture* business. They would know what it was to look into the eyes of The Other. There would always be someone who remembered their birthday; they'd possess a reasonable idea of what they looked like from behind. Everything that is missing would come together. Everything would be whole.

Sarah and I used to take baths together when we were small. She was afraid of the end with the drain, afraid she was going to get sucked down it and into the netherworld of her nightmares. My brothers encouraged her in this, teasing her by pursing their lips together and making deep sucking sounds. At that sound, I could see the fear come into her face, I could hear the sounds of self-congratulatory delight in my brothers' shrieks, and if I'd been just a bit older, my external social choices would have been clear: Side with her and tell them to stop, or side with them and tease her even more. But I had my own watery-abyss nightmares to deal with, and my actual choice was this: Be Just Like Her, or not. I took a deep breath and slid my naked body over toward that dangerously fascinating hole.

The difference in Sarah's twinhood and mine from that of other twinhoods has not so much to do with what happened to me when I was nine, when I got jaw cancer, but with the story I told about it afterward, the book I wrote about growing up with a face different from everyone else's. My publisher sent me from bookstore to bookstore to give readings, and after each reading came a question-and-answer period. Soon, I learned to expect the question: 'You say so little about your twin sister. Why is that?'

This could be asked with a tone of concern – obviously I was not in touch with an important aspect of my psyche. Or it could be asked with something approaching accusation: I was withholding obviously critical information from them.

I could never, or at least not in the arena of the podium of a crowded bookstore, get across to my inquisitor that the real story is that there is no story, at least not the one they're looking for, the simple story of parts that click together and create a pleasing, distinguishable form. I can't blame them. Who wouldn't want such a story?

My mother and father, who already had three well-grown children by the time Sarah and I arrived, always introduced us with 'and this is Sarah and Lucy.' When we were instructed to do things, it was 'Sarah and Lucy come here, Sarah and Lucy go to bed, Sarah and Lucy, time to eat your dinner.' Accustomed to distinguishing themselves from others, familiar with separation both in label and, often all too painfully, in life, this was a natural and convenient way to speak to and about us. No one thought much about it until one day, I don't know how young I was, someone asked me while I was alone what my name was. I responded, so I am told, that my name was Sarah and Lucy.

The surrealist Magritte produced a few canvases involving themselves with language and image. One of the paintings depicted a series of items rendered in a mode of 'realism' and then labeled, in words painted directly below each item, as either not what it appeared to be ('this is not a pipe') or something entirely other than what the image would be commonly thought to represent (a horse designated as a door).

On one level, this is just the simple embodiment of language and aesthetic theories that any undergraduate can apprehend, the now familiar exercise of discerning that the staple activities of seeing and labeling, tools we employ to understand the world around us, are just that, tools, nothing more, and might even be based on rather more arbitrary systems than we first suspected. Intelligence is based on this facility – to be able, first, to distinguish one thing from another thing, and then, once the 'thing' (usually a process or idea) is identified, to go on and recognize that with the 'thing' now named, discerned, it can be further examined, analyzed, categorized; in essence, 'made' to mean.

The trouble with this sort of intelligence, to the delight of critics and the betterment of astute politicians since the beginning of time, is the inherent tendency to forget that identifying processes is itself a process. Even while perspicaciously and fervently seeing the world around us, it is extremely difficult to actually see ourselves seeing the world. Intellectually, we can examine only the thought we *just* had, not the thought we are in the moment having about that previous thought. If we are lucky, we grow more and more acquainted and hopefully comfortable with this flow. We learn that one idea, one notion of how the world works, is bound to be turned over for the next idea, the next notion, and that nothing we can talk about in language and with reason is permanently fixed, is rigidly true. If we are not lucky, we are overly susceptible to other people's pet processes and, most dangerously, their ideologies.

Ultimately, Magritte's painting defuses any ideology or theory that can be formed over time around it even while it itself is a fixed object in time. It does this simply by being a painting (*'This is not an idea'*), relying on the artificiality that art is, after all, named after. Amid the misnamed images in his paintings, there is in fact one, a suitcase, that is 'properly' named. In the process of all this naming going on, it is inevitable that something, or someone, gets it right every once in a while. Though we have moments of understanding, who we think we are is not permanently fixed, and who we think we should be is not rigidly true.

One thing that intrigues both scientists and sensationalists alike is the idea that twins are sometimes known to form their own secret languages. There is a story in my family about Susie and the Spider. Susie is our older sister and for a short while, when we were only two and Susie was eight, the three of us shared a room together.

The point of the family story is that a spider was crawling on the wall near Susie's head while she was still asleep. Sarah and I woke her and pointed it out and, much to our entertainment, Susie started screaming so loud my mother had to run in and capture the spider in a pair of Susie's underwear, which in her panic she then threw out the window.

Another part of the story, though, is that Sarah and I clearly remember being awake in our cribs next to each other for a long time before we woke Susie, discussing the various options at our disposal. It was a complex discussion, involving many conjectures and much reasoning and, in retrospect, was far more subtle and thorough than our English language abilities at the time could have possibly allowed. We remember that discussion very clearly, but we have no memory of what tongue we actually spoke it in. If we did not have each other to verify that this conversation actually took place, if would be easy to ascribe various tricks of memory as an explanation to believing something that otherwise couldn't possibly be true.

I never tell people this part of the story. I never tell it because I don't know what it means, I don't know what *really* happened, and I know that other people, not just people who aren't twins but people who just simply *aren't* me, would immediately assume that they did.

Mary Shelley's *Frankenstein* can be seen as the story of a doppelgänger. In this instance, the doppelgänger isn't a natural product of nature (and as such an example of the implicit duality of nature), but an actual creation of Frankenstein, of man. Everything we make, everything we do, is an emanation of who we are, both the good and the bad. If we mess around with nature too much, messing around with it here being equal to attempting to understand and mimic it, things end up badly, evil, even.

My face, the lower half of it anyway, is a made thing. A partial mandiblectomy and years of reconstructive surgery have completely shorn from me an image of what my face was 'supposed' to look like. It's taken me this long into the writing of this essay to bring this up as an issue because I don't *want* people to think that what my twin sister really represents for me is the alternative version of the person I'd have become, or at least looked like, had I never had cancer. I don't want this to be part of my story, her story, our story. Partly, this is denial that something tragic happened to me, but mostly it is my innate knowledge that the story (the story of my having a twin) is really about something very different from what other people think it is about. I cannot articulate exactly what it is about, at least not with the language I have, not with the process of thinking about it which I employ at this moment, but I don't want people to step into this perceived gap and fill it with their own ideas and theories.

When we were about ten my father bought me a stuffed gorilla while I was in the hospital and told me not to tell Sarah because she might get jealous. Not long after I got home, I just couldn't keep it to myself any more.

'You see this gorilla? Daddy gave this to me and he told me not to tell you because he wasn't giving you one.'

We were in the middle of some gathering fight that had not yet erupted, but the tension was there. This bit of gorilla information seemed like the perfect weapon against, or actually for, the display of anger I knew was coming. Sarah has big, obvious buttons that were easy to press and I loved to press them, to see the sparks fly. Temperamentally, we've always been almost eerily dissimilar to each other. I was calm and slow to anger; Sarah was the proverbial fire-cracker. I was brave; Sarah was a scaredy-cat. I liked to be alone; Sarah was social. I was very quiet; Sarah was talkative.

I threw this gorilla grenade at her and, to my surprise, rather than yelling at me, hitting me, storming out of the room, she was quiet. She looked at me with her big open blue eyes, eyes almost but not just like mine, and I watched them start to fill with tears. She looked at me as if she had never seen me before, and, in doing so, offered an image of herself, and of myself, that I had never seen before. For most of my life I'd been trying to hurt Sarah, get back at Sarah, provoke Sarah, and for most of her life she'd been trying to do the same to me. Now, for the first time, I saw that I affected Sarah. The curtains were yellow and I noticed they were blowing in the window, and the usual clutter on the floor was the usual clutter, but somehow I recognized it as being part of the scene, part of the room I was in, part of the life I was living. Sarah was part of this life too, part of my life, but for the first time I consciously registered her as having her own life, her own version of herself, her own version of me. The room was quiet except for the gentle rasping sound the curtains made against the windowsill and the obnoxious snorting the dog was making as she suddenly felt the need to chew on her leg. Something had just happened, but neither one of us knew what. We sat there and stared at each other until the next everyday thing happened and drew us back, yet again, into our separate lives.

Sarah is ten minutes younger than I am, making me the older sister, something I lorded over her for years. Until I was seven or eight, it seemed perfectly logical to both of us that when I died, Sarah would automatically die ten minutes later. We tried to come up with complex plans about how she could be notified immediately upon my death – walkie-talkies? – and so know she had exactly ten minutes left. If I was ever jealous of Sarah, it was for this; I wanted to be the one to have my life filled with such sudden, however brief, urgency. At night, I used to lie in the bed, the twin bed, next to hers and imagine such a momentous gift.

From the beginning I knew I would write this essay about how my sister did not mean for me the things other people told me she should. The essay, then, wanted to be about this lack, about how meaning resists the molds we want to pour it into. But that was what the essay wanted; what I wanted turned out to be something very different. Without even knowing it, I wanted this essay to transform my relationship with my sister into something extraordinary; my very unknowing about my sister could transform into a knowing if only I wrote about it. *This is my sister*. Even now, as I type, this essay wants me to render my sister in precise terms, wants my desire to take on the shape of something that vaguely resembles me. *This is not my sister*. But what I know, and what the world and even this essay do not, is that this essay is really about how I can't have a twin, I can't. Because if I did, wouldn't everything be different? There can't be a correlation between me and Sarah because if there was, how could the world leave me to experience the moments of intense loneliness that I do? How could that be? How could the world, my sister, this essay, leave me high and dry like that?

I remember once walking to elementary school with Sarah. We did this every day for years, cutting through backyards with dogs standing up on the ends of their chains, barking. One day we walked through the leaves of late autumn, wet leaves because it had rained all night, me turning over the reams of leaves to search for earthworms beneath them. I loved the dark world of the soil, the intricate, unfathomable lives of bugs. Sarah did not. The sky was growing darker; it looked like it might rain again in the next hour.

Why these moments overtake us I don't know, but there was something about the different types of darkness layering themselves around me: dark sky, dark leaves, dark soil, and then the whiteness of the birch trees' bark, the whiteness of Sarah's pale Irish skin. I looked at Sarah and realized that I did not know who she was. I looked at her and said, in full astonishment, 'You're my sister. You're my sister.' I didn't know exactly what I was feeling, though I did know it wasn't completely unpleasant. 'You're my sister,' I said for several minutes on end, which is how long it took for the high, disassociated feeling to pass. I was naming it for myself more than telling her, astounded not by her, but by the bizarre, random oddity of the fact. 'Oh shut up already,' she finally said, annoyed, possibly scared of my behavior. 'Who the hell else would I be?'

Later, I told on her for saying 'hell'.

THE GIRLS

'GIIIRRRL: YOU DO LOOK fine.'

In truth, Lisa did not look fine. Black half moons shone dimly beneath her eyes, and the foundation she had wiped thick as salve upon them only made it worse. It brought to mind those Band-Aids that pretend to be the color of skin. The black circles weren't bruises – no one had hit her or anything – they were simply the aftermath of her life as she'd lived it, tick by tick, up until that very moment. Deb knew that Lisa did not look fine, but still, the response was part of the rote, and as Lisa stepped into the living room in her black minidress, she looked at us expectantly.

'Girl, you sure do look fine,' Carl agreed with Deb. Carl was not in drag, but still had the accent. Why do all the drag queens I meet speak with this accent? Is cross-dressing a place you have to live in, a region with its own colloquial vowels?

When I am in England, which I visit often because of London-dwelling siblings, I avoid speaking for as long as possible while in public places. Not just because I fear being found out as an alien, but also there is the very real possibility of suddenly blurting out a half-assed English accent myself. Nothing is more mortifying. I've seen it happen to others. The rhythms just soak into you; you can't help it.

Here, I avoid speaking as well. Not that these people are

about to mistake me for one of their own. It's the early 1980's and I am in college and, so far, have successfully avoided sex my entire life. And even as I wear my hair very short, avoid any clothing remotely feminine, and run when my friends turn to me with their bottles of makeup, I do take a certain, quiet pride in being the genuine article, the thing they are all imitating. I think. I mean, it's not that I wear rubber minidresses, or even wish to. I'm not a femme fatale, or at least not yet, and even then will never be as good as they are.

'Come here and let me touch that dress,' Carl says, blowing a straight, hurried line of smoke out his mouth. Carl isn't going out tonight because he's leaving for Florida on the early flight. A job interview, I think, but I'm not sure. In the kitchen, earlier that evening, he told me about the flight in a tone of voice that let me know I was supposed to already understand these details. I nodded my head and dodged my ignorance with an offering of the tale of my first and definitely last visit to Disney World in Orlando. A lot of ear paraphernalia, I explained.

Lisa walks over and permits Carl to finger the material.

'Is this Dior, or De Or?'

'Same to you, sweetie,' Lisa replies with a smile. The joke has something to do with a hybrid of New Yorkese 'Dese, Dem, and Dose' lingo, and a play on the idea that the dress is other, or 'Or', than an actual Christian Dior. I think. I tried to pick things up as I went along. Cynicism, I did know, was the basic grammar.

Soon enough, Lisa and Deb leave for the club near 43rd Street. Carl goes home to pack. I go home alone, declining offers from both sides. Somehow I knew either place would ultimately depress me.

I hung out with drag queens because I thought they were exotic. Their exoticism transferred a title of cool upon me, without my actually having to do very much except sit around on endless couches in cramped apartments and offer ignored opinions on clothes, hair, and makeup. I felt safe there. Hanging out with mall shoppers from Westchester – the other breed of female whose ludicrous ideas of what it was to be female once held out threats simply because I came of age among them – was something I considered beneath me, so instead, and in revenge, I hung with their evil twins, the drag queens of Manhattan. Both consumed equal amounts of hair spray and mascara. Both lived out an interpretation of what it was to be female that had nothing to do with me, the so-called genuine article.

I hated fairy tales as a child because they had nothing to do with reality. Not because they spoke of goblins and elves and giants, not because of such obvious unreality. It had more to do with their neatly packaged morals. Mostly, I hated the notion that you got what you deserved. As I understood life, you rarely got what you deserved, and if you did, you'd better start looking over your shoulder. How could anyone hold such a romantic, naïve idea about the world that outlined such a ludicrous notion?

Of course, I'm speaking of the sterilized version of fairy tales most of America's youth are subjected to: the flat-chested Snow White and her clownish dwarfs; the gnomish Rumpelstiltskin, whose evilness is de facto because of his ugliness. It never occurred to me to wonder what desperate loneliness drove Rumpelstiltskin to so covet a first-born child of his own, or what brand of cultural and personal narcissism fueled Cinderella's belief that the reward for perseverance through hardship was material wealth. I just somehow understood they were wrong.

If I'd been allowed to read the unabridged versions, the Grimms' tales of ambiguous rewards and even the darkly punishing tales of Hans Christian Andersen – magic shoes that dance your feet to bloody stubs, mermaids who give up everything magical for an unrequited and lackluster reality – I might have later understood better the lives of my perverted friends. As it was, I spent time with Deb and Lisa and Carl, a.k.a. Carol, because they glittered, and because I wanted to walk away with some of that glitter upon me without ever actually having to take responsibility for it. I could imagine myself a femme fatale all evening, an underground literary curiosity, but still wake up intact in the morning. No midnight-pumpkin curfews for me, no regrets that perhaps that frog hadn't been a prince after all. I could take of all their feminine desires, all their fairy-tale beliefs that it was just a matter of trying and primping hard enough, and walk away clean.

Four o'clock in the morning: a loud banging on my dormitory door. I'm dreaming about sailing – I hate sailing – and the captain's menacing orders, the waves banging, the storm approaching, all blend into one and arrive at my door.

'Let me in! It's an emergency!' I recognize Deb's voice.

Seriously doubting it's an emergency, because it never is, I get up and unlock the door.

'I must have money,' Deb announces, sitting down on my bed. Typically, almost cartoonishly, she opens her purse and takes out her compact and lipstick.

'What do you need money for?' I ask, taking the bait.

Deb launches into a story about how Lisa's has been arrested for soliciting, and she, Deb, is raising bail money. I tell her I don't have any, which is the truth. Almost the truth. I have a hundred-dollar bill hidden in a book, John Berryman's *The Dream Songs*, on my shelf. I feel guilty for not telling Deb, but I also know from experience I'd never see that money again if I did tell her. It's not that she's dishonest; she just doesn't seem to keep tabs on things the way most people do.

Still, I feel guilty. Lisa's been arrested before, I tell myself, and she always gets out of it. It's not like we're that close or anything. It's the only money I've got, I tell myself. Deb walks away with the sixteen dollars I had in my wallet.

Lisa's arrest will be only one more minor diversion on the road to who she 'really is'. She works the streets once in awhile both because she likes having that power over men and because the money is good. Her taste in clothes is expensive, as are all of her friends. I'm a regular ragamuffin next to them. To them, what they desire constitutes accurate projections of who they really are. In this way, they're no different from hardly anyone else. If they can refine their desires to recognize only the best, that is proof enough that they themselves are the best.

'I'm going to get me a Porsche, honey, and then you'll be sorry.'

'Porsche? Girl, you *are* just new money trash. Got to have a Jaguar. Only way to go.'

'You're all wrong: a Mercedes convertible, two-door, forest green.'

At this point in my life I put up with this metaphysical foolishness because my own sexual life is so hidden and tortured. It's a trade-off: I get to watch them in all their fabricated glory, and they get to be watched. My friends have enough sexuality to go around, and I lap it up, knowing I can do so at my own pace. This isn't true around 'real' women, because they offer the image of what I am not, and it isn't true around 'real' men, because all they offer is what I can't have.

Despite all the sterilized, Disney-fied versions of fairy tales that presented themselves to me throughout my childhood, one original story, in all its oddness, did find its way to my doorstep: Hans Christian Andersen's 'The Girl Who Trod on a Loaf'.

Basically, it's the tale of a girl who was a rather horrid little girl; she loved to pull the wings off flies, and was so vain that rather than ruin her shoes, she preferred to throw down a loaf of bread on the ground and use it as a stepping-stone. The loaf was intended for her hungry mother, and when the girl stepped on the now ruined and muddy loaf, she sank down into the lair of the Marsh Woman. There, she was traded off to the Bogeyman's mother, who wanted to use her as a statue in her own home. The girl who trod on the loaf was doomed then to stand motionless, hungry, and unhappy in the cold, dark chamber.

Three things struck me most about this tale: One, once a statue, the girl was tormented by flies who crawled all over her and could not fly away because their wings had been plucked off. Two, the girl could actually hear all the tales and songs written about her fate up above, in the land she'd once inhabited. Three, she herself never actually escaped; eventually, she transformed into a bird that flew up to the world and did its own version of good, but she herself, as an actual little girl, was gone for ever.

There's no easy way to interpret this story. I do know that the author's subtle touch regarding the flies chilled me to the bone. Up until that moment in life I'd embarked on a good amount of insect torture of my own. This story stopped me dead in my tracks. It had nothing to do with my having been turned into a 'good' person; simply, I was afraid I'd suffer the same fate. It was transformation of the inner self not through good intent, but morbid fear.

That the girl could hear the stories and songs made up about her plight touched me in a far less precise way. As if we want to be the heroes of our own stories at whatever cost. And then, to go through all that suffering, only to transform into something that, while beautiful and airy, could not possibly fully enjoy the freedom in exactly the way the girl had desired it. Or could it? Does the thing we are always trying to transform into, the thing we most desire to be, *have* to cast off what it once was, is that the whole point?

Though there wasn't anything *overtly* sexual in this or any of the other fairy tales I read, there was something *deeply* sexual about them, an underground troll kind of sexuality that lived beneath the bridge you had to walk over on your way to the rest of your life. At any moment, it could grab you. As an adolescent, my deep fear of sex could be matched only by my deeper interest. I thought that sex, once undertaken, was the thing that transformed you for ever and ever and ever. There wouldn't be any coming back, any godmothers to uncast the spell. Because I was too afraid to cross that bridge for myself until I was into my twenties, I watched my friends cross it for me. These particular friends not only crossed it, they jumped into the river.

Lisa wants me to write something about her. That's the hitch to being a writer among theatrical people: They are all looking for good parts.

'I got a million stories, sweetie, and they could be yours,' Lisa winks at me. She thinks the way it works is that I will pay her for her stories.

'Who do you want to play you when they make the movie?' Carol asks.

'Oh, lord, who else but Dolly Parton?' Lisa says, adjusting her breasts.

'She's not an actress, she's a singer,' Carol rejoins, but it's too late, Lisa is already singing 'Nine to Five' and shimmying up against the doorway. All of my favorite drag queens love doorways. Their lives center around entrances and exits, and when you absolutely must stick around, they tell me, try to do it in a doorway. Life as an eternal passage.

My own femininity is lurking in another doorway. Once in

a while, if I turn quickly enough, I can almost see myself as I will be in only a year or two's time, loitering suggestively in a short black dress. You see, soon I'll graduate, go to the Midwest to earn yet another degree, and change into an entirely different person. I'll abandon one version of myself, only to throw myself with abandon into the next self. I'll make up for lost time. I'll grow my hair long and learn the fangledness of garter belts. And jealousy. And the unabridged versions of the old-time sadnesses – the stories I thought would disappear. Though I'll never get to the point of false eyelashes, for a few years I will wear my new sexuality as carefully and protectively as I once wore my asexuality. I will learn to style my hair and dance in high heels. The transformation will be so complete that my old friends will almost not recognize me when I return for a visit. Much later, two of them will be dead from AIDS.

But for now, of course, none of us knows just how the story will turn out.

'Well, isn't it just little Miss Cinderella!' Deb declares as I walk into the apartment in a tight minidress, a whole summer later.

'Girl, I hear you been getting it till you're raw!' Lisa screams, much to my embarrassment. It's true, I'd recently, finally, lost my virginity.

'Tell us all about him,' Deb says.

Though in truth the guy is a loser, they're all looking at me expectantly, pulling out their packs of cigarettes in anticipation. So I tell a version of the tale anyway; not exactly the true tale, but a small true part of the tale, a version in which I get what I want, and what I want turns out to be exactly who I am. My friends coo, over all of us, long into the night.

THE YELLOW HOUSE

OFF THE THRUWAY JUST east of the Tappan Zee Bridge, there used to be a wooden yellow house set back about a quarter of a mile from the highway. I think the first time I noticed this house was when I was eleven, on the drive to Sarah Lawrence College, where we were about to deliver my older sister, Suellen, who attended Sarah Lawrence between 1975 and 1979. College had such a grown-up air to it, and in my mind this yellow house became entangled with the drive to the college, and with all those grown-up things I understood must be taking place at college. When it was announced, toward the end of a long weekend, that it was time to drive Suellen back to college, my father might as well have announced we were driving her to some distant galaxy.

The yellow house had an elegant white porch that ran along two sides of it, and a gray tiled roof. The house had a turret, too, which piqued my imagination, because there weren't too many turrets, or even porches for that matter, in my own neighborhood. Where I lived the houses were all similar to one another – rectangular, mid-sized, and not actually painted in the way I somehow thought houses should be painted, where you could see wide-bristle brushstrokes on the wood. Our houses instead were built out of some sturdy, peculiar, corrugated material, material that had a Venus-born-fully-formed look to it, an uncanny, untouched feel to it. Our house was pale green, and there was no sign of human influence, of a manual application of color, anywhere on it. I know because I looked; the summer sun made the driveway shimmer like water in the distance as I ran my eyes over my house's surface, searching.

This mystified me when I was very young. I kept trying to figure out how they got the color into the material and why it never seemed to fade or peel or blister, why our house never seemed to need a new coat of paint, as I imagined the yellow house did, though I couldn't actually see this for sure because the yellow house was too far from the road to make out such details.

But what really offended me about my green house, and about all the houses in the neighborhood, was that all of them had fake shutters nailed on to the exterior wall alongside each window. For the longest time I never understood why we all allowed pseudo, useless shutters on our houses, but what flabbergasted me most of all was that everyone went on with their lives regardless. All those birthday parties in backyards, all those fathers washing their cars in the driveway, all those wives balancing the groceries on their knees as they unlocked their front doors. Not one person, as far as I could see, ever stopped dead in his tracks to stare in horrified amazement at his house, recognizing not just the ridiculousness, but the sadness, and the strange vanity, of those impotent shutters.

Apart from its quaintness, and apart from its 'realness' (the shutters on the yellow house had to be real, of this I was certain), what captivated me most about the yellow house was that it was literally on the precipice of a great void. Some company had bought up the land the house sat on and had commenced digging a gigantic hole right next to it. It was a huge hole, taking up ten times the space the house did; presumably it was to be the basement of some big office building, and the yellow house, obviously empty, sat precariously on the edge. After the company dug the hole, they must have gone bankrupt, because the hole was as far as construction ever got. The whole site remained abandoned for years.

All of this, though, sat at the back of my mind; I didn't think about it so much as experience it. Each time we'd drive by the yellow house I'd picture myself sitting in the turret of such a house, living a life of high teas and bawdy arguments about aesthetics with bearded men over glasses of sherry, which, I imagined, must taste like cherries. The life I invented for myself in that house was a grand life, yet also an honest and pure life, and I fantasized about how I'd grow up, become rich, and buy the yellow house and the land, fill up that big hole. I myself would attend college, that mystical place, and I'd invite all my fascinating friends over to discuss our latest trip down the Nile, interspersing descriptions of affairs with the handsome guide later eaten tragically by lions with our newest plan to save the world's suffering poor, the starving millions. It was a house of pure heroism and romance, a childish house inhabited by my invented adult self.

My actual adult self began making sporadic appearances in my life as I became a teenager, and the messages she bore from the future were just as idealized as before, but now also came with strange cryptic inferences about how it might all be a bit more complicated and banal than I'd previously imagined. Eventually it was time to go to college, and I applied to and was accepted at Sarah Lawrence.

I had seen the yellow house the previous spring when I'd gone to the college for my admission interview. I hadn't thought about the yellow house in a long time, but there it was, still on the brink. Then, when my mother drove me, boxes crammed in the backseat, up the thruway to actually move into the college that next fall, I looked over toward the house. Something financial must have happened, another company must have bought the land, because just as I looked over, at precisely that moment, a large wrecking ball the size of a car crashed into the yellow house and sent half of it sliding down into the long-patient hole. The standing half sat there forlornly in the rising dust, a bisected doll's house. Through the dust I could now, finally, see the rooms I'd wondered about so long ago. They were all empty of furniture and smaller than I'd imagined.

It was the coincidence of it that floored me then, the question of what possible puppeteer of convergent fate had nudged my gaze in that exact direction at that exact moment. If I hadn't looked just then, it's possible the office would have been built and become part of the landscape and it might very well have taken me years to figure out that the yellow house was gone. It had to mean something, I felt, had to refer to or validate some larger scheme of meaning, this dramatic little signifier. That special moment with the yellow house meant something, I was sure, though I couldn't for the life of me figure out exactly what.

I spent childhood obsessed with details. The direction of the wood grain in tables, the particular creaks of each chair – each of these was just as, if not more, important to me than the people who sat down to those tables; it was, in fact, my way of avoiding whoever sat down at those tables of my childhood. The hair on the back of a doctor's hands, or the way anger took form in my mother's lipstick, flaking on the corner of her mouth. When I was sick in bed, I loved the dust in the sunlight, the metallic smell of sunlight itself, the shush of sheets pushed aside. When other people were cruel to me, I took note of the way their coats flapped in the wind as they ran, the space between their front teeth, the way the butter melted on the toast I ate while sitting alone at home afterward. I loved light most of all, especially because it could always surprise me, winking at me from windows as I turned my head, softly glowing from the back of my father's head as he drove, soaking into the blood of a dead animal spread out like some map on the dark asphalt road.

Learning to observe the world's details was my way of avoiding it. When I went to college, that galaxy where everything was suddenly supposed to matter, I learned, for the first time, that observation could become a way to enter the world. In other words, I began writing. The ability to see was no longer passive; it was a tool to create doorways leading toward the larger connotations in life. In *The Seventh Seal*, Max von Sydow sits there in a field holding a bowl of strawberries and milk, asking out loud what the meaning of life is. The answer is right there in Sydow's hands, but there is no way to say this and have it make sense, so instead the director, Ingmar Bergman, lets the answer sit there, waiting to be noticed by either the blessed or the educated viewer. That bouquet of details, that small bowlful of particulars – it's as much truth as can be packed into one long glance while sitting in a dark theater, and then it's passed and you have to go looking for the next answer.

Because writing was my way of both doubting and adoring the world, my own private religion, I should have known that something strange was bound to happen when I put my own life under the microscope of my writing. My childhood had taught me that the terrors of actual mirrors were nothing compared with the terrors of mirrors I falsely placed on other people's perception of me. I thought that self-fulfillment could be found only through other people's approval of what I looked like, and it took me years to figure out that I had somehow allowed society's idea of what I should look like to merge with *my* ideas of what I should look like, that I'd allowed it to cover my own identity with a mask I mistook for reality. It took me years to figure out how to separate the two. Writing helped me in this; it showed me the true direction of a mirror, which is always pointed back to the self. With all this knowledge about mirrors, why was I so unprepared for the next mirror, the rather elaborate and gilded one created by the media?

When I was twenty-nine, a friend asked me to write an essay for an anthology she was putting together. I'd been wanting to write about my childhood experience of cancer and disfigurement for a while but needed an outside push like this for me to sit down finally and do it. While writing the essay, the first essay I had written since college and my very first personal essay, I agonized about two things. The first was, since I knew all the material so well, I feared it was boring. The other difficulty was trying to make it all make sense: How do you, after all, come up with a thesis statement about your own life? I kept wanting to come up with the grand summation but luckily, in the nick of time, realized that the only thing to do was to be honest: I hadn't come up with the grand plan, the final realm of understanding. I told the story as best I could and then fessed up: Sometimes I thought I knew what it meant; other times I didn't. It was that same wavering between the real and the abstract again, and, as a writer, my only job (and what a relief) was to convey that doubt. Just to make sure, though, I ended the essay with a concrete image.

An agent who looked at the anthology gave me a call, and before I knew it, because it all happened in about ten days, I was the proud, somewhat bewildered owner of a contract to write my memoir. I wrote the book, handed it in, and then had to go on a book tour. My very first 'gig' was at a TV station in Connecticut, and I was put on a train. As it happened, I missed the right station and had to backtrack, making me very late. My media escort (a job I didn't even know existed until then) met me at the station, and we sped down to the television building, then literally ran through the hallways, trying to make the live show on time. We reached the right studio and had to sneak in. It was a large room, some four or five thousand square feet. Most of it was darkened, and in each corner I could see the set for what must be different segments of the show, which was a daytime talk/variety show. There was the kitchen for the cooking segment; the oblong desk and blank, green weather map for the news segment; two stools set up in front of a huge, fake picture window, presumably for the chat segments; and then my two hosts, a man and a woman, sitting in the lit-up part of the studio on a couch in what I presumed was meant to look like a living room.

Except for a brief appearance on *Romper Room* when I was in kindergarten, and a visit to the news room where my father worked when I was about eight (I got to sit in Walter Cronkite's chair; big thrill), this was my first time in a television studio as an adult. For weeks beforehand, I'd wondered how I would hold up, afraid that I'd faint from fear. This first day, I walked gingerly in and sat down in the dark, watching as the two hosts read their TelePrompters under the bright lights. They were, as I'd anticipated, incredibly fake in their mannerisms. When they talked, they used their features in exaggerated ways, and emphasized rhythms in their speech that made them sound stilted. I guess I'd expected that.

What I didn't expect was that after they announced a commercial, after the screens went up in the control room and down on the set, my hosts would turn to me and, in exactly the same strangely nuanced voices, stuffed with false familiarity, comment that it must have been 'that nasty weather' that made me late. A little bewildered, I was led up to the couch, where I sat still while a sound man fussed over my mike.

'I just *loved* your book,' the woman told me with a great, rubbery grin and a curious, downward flip of her hands.

So shocked that I didn't even care enough to be nervous for the cameras, I looked at both their heavily made up faces and asked, 'Do you really talk like this?' Maybe I was being rude, but I was so genuinely surprised that they didn't 'turn it off' when the camera's red light wasn't lit. Just then the headphoned floor manager started counting down until airtime. I looked off to the side, where I caught a sudden glimpse of myself on camera. Instinctively knowing it would be better that way, I decided to turn my head away.

'So, when was the first time you looked in a mirror and realized you felt ugly?'

This wasn't the first question, but it was only a three-minute interview, so it must have come early. I'd anticipated questions about how I'd come to write the book, technical questions like that. Nothing quite like this. And because I was new to the game, sucker that I was, I actually tried to answer this question.

'Well, there wasn't any *first* moment, or even one moment.' I paused to think. I felt stumped. 'It sort of happened more gradually; it was more like a lot of little moments that accumulated?' I offered. I don't think I was making all that much sense. In the end, and I was to discover this held true for most television, making sense didn't actually matter, just plain talking did, and if I could save them from any 'dead air', my hosts were invariably pleased with me.

This was just the beginning of a book tour that lasted over a year. As long as I was careful never to read, listen to, or, most important, watch any of my interviews, I enjoyed the whole process, even when I was exhausted by it. A love of irony is important in life, and I well understood the strangeness of *me*, of all people, becoming the subject of all those fashion photo shoots, of being a guest of a famous supermodel on her trendy MTV show about style. People often remarked how confident I seemed. I guess I'd always suspected, but now I knew for sure: I was a ham. What people didn't know was that I restricted my awareness to the present moment. I enjoyed being treated like such a character, and I enjoyed the fable of 'poor little disfigured girl makes good', and as long as I stayed entirely in the moment, which is to say as long as I didn't look at the results (the photo, the interview, etc.), I was free to enjoy myself. One look at myself on TV, and I'd probably have turned into a neurotic mess.

I was interviewed well over a hundred times about the book. Contrary to what I'd feared, a large number of people 'got it', which is to say they understood that the book wasn't so much about cancer and disfigurement as it was about self: about how we define ourselves, how we seek out things and people in the world to tell us who we are. But a lot of people didn't get it, and the more I was interviewed, the more I came to appreciate a 'good' interviewer, someone who was actually willing to engage in a true dialogue. A 'bad' interviewer asked questions such as 'What's it *like* to have cancer?' or 'You write a lot about X; can you tell me about X?'

The problem with the latter question is that I've already said it all in the book, so why would I possibly want to say more about it, while the first question is bad because it's just too sweeping. Having cancer is not *like* anything; it *is* what I've already written about in the book. I'd guess roughly half of my interviewers hadn't actually read the book.

Maybe I was getting tired and just a tad grouchy, but toward the end of the tour I noticed a definite urge to scream when asked either of these questions. If I'd written a novel or any other nonfiction book, I could have done what most of my other writer friends do – get your stock answers memorized and simply go on automatic pilot. Unfortunately, this was my own life I was talking about, and I could never get over the desire to *get it right*, to set the record straight.

As time wore on, I began to understand particular patterns to my sudden so-called fame. Originally, before it all started, I was afraid of being asked too many questions about my face; I didn't want to get bogged down by the physical details of my story. As it turned out, I was surprised at how many people were willing to talk about the more metaphysical aspects of my face; yet, at the same time, many people seemed desperate for me to symbolize something. My story, I quickly found out, was all about how 'beauty is really on the inside', about 'how it doesn't matter what you look like', how 'society puts too much emphasis on looks'.

'What message would you like readers to come away from your book with?' Countless times this question was thrown at me. And each and every time I'd have to answer, 'There is no message. My book is about my life: How can a life have a message? You just simply live it.'

The worst questions were those that begged a truism, a platitude, a cliché for the answer. 'Wouldn't you say that the fashion industry puts too much emphasis on the way women look?' They wanted me to agree, to place blame, and it would have been easier, but instead, each and every time I felt I had to say, 'Of course they do; that's their job, that's what fashion *is*. I'm not here to tell people to stop wanting to be beautiful.' No matter how tired I was of the same question, I had to enter into the dialogue with each interviewer, I had to redefine for them who I was, because I'd come to realize that the aesthetic behind this type of questioning underscored the very aesthetic I'd had to reject in the first place simply in order to survive my ordeal. What they wanted was to place me between the pages of gorgeous models in magazines that were all about how terribly important beauty was, and to have my story stand for the opposite camp. What I didn't understand for the longest time, what I couldn't understand until I was so relentlessly questioned about it, is that, ultimately, the two opposing camps become the same thing.

It's not the idea that 'beauty only truly comes from within' which I objected to; it's the platitudinous way the interviewers wanted me to say it. Anything put into the form of a truism immediately, and paradoxically, becomes false simply because it is so neatly packaged – as neatly and insidiously packaged as the model on the page across from my interview trying to sell self-confidence in the form of a cellulite reducer. Most educated people know that a cellulite reducer will not give them happiness, but not every educated person knows that clichés about inner beauty won't show them the way either. What's more, it's mostly educated women who are *buying* that cellulite cream. Why? Because human beings are that smart and that dumb at the same time. The danger of the 'neat package,' whether it's skin cream or catchy sayings, is that it doesn't allow for complicated, often conflicting, responses toward things. Somewhere along the line we become convinced that the goal is to have clear feelings and harmonious ideas about things, to be able to verbally ask what is the meaning of all this and expect a grammatically correct answer, rather than allow for the fact that the answer might be constructed of a completely different syntax and idiom, like Max von Sydow's strawberries.

What does the yellow house have to do with all this? The best answer might be in the both perfect and sloppy form of a poem by John Berryman. Berryman wrote a series of poems he called *The Dream Songs*, and these were mostly poems three stanzas long, and mostly 'starred' a character named Henry, a doppelgänger for Berryman. Berryman often made both obvious and obscure cultural references without explaining them, such as some of the movie references below, and he also frequently adopted a 'hip' or 'beat' syntax and/or spelling (he wasn't exactly a beat poet, but he was close enough) of words. The word *Fúnnee* below is such a use/spelling of the word *funny*.

'The Prisoner of Shark Island' with Paul Muni

Henry is old, old; for Henry remembers
Mr Deeds' tuba, & the Cameo,
& the race in *Ben Hur, – The Lost World*, with sound,
& *The Man from Blankley's*, which he did not dig,
nor did he understand one caption of,
bewildered Henry, while the Big Ones laughed.

Now Henry is unmistakenly a Big One.
Fúnnee; he don't feél so.
He just stuck around.
The German & the Russian films into
Italian & Japanese films turned, while many
were prevented from making it.

He wishing he could squirm again where Hoot
is just ahead of rustlers, where William S
forgoes some deep advantage, & moves on,
where Hashknife Hartly having the matter taped
the rats are flying. For the rats
have moved in, mostly, and this is for real.

On a simple level, the first stanza is 'about' a child watching movies, some of which are over his head, and the last stanza is 'about', after having grown up, wishing for the ordered world of those movies once more, a world where the danger was pretend rather than real. (I put the word *about* in quotation marks because, to paraphrase the poet Heather McHugh, most poems are actually *about* about.)

It's the second stanza that is the key. The first stanza is about grown-ups laughing at jokes in a movie that a child doesn't understand. In the second stanza, in the first line, Henry grows up. But the altered use of the word *funny* in the second line echoes back to those laughing adults, and even though Henry is unmistakenly grown up, he still doesn't 'get' it, get what the others seem to understand. As children, we believe that someday we will be told the secrets we're sure adults hold, that we will be handed the necessary knowledge to 'get' life. There's a sense that there's something we have to *do* to become adults, but all Henry does is stick around; he's helpless to fate. And while on one level the changing of the German and Russian films into Italian and Japanese films lets us know that time is passing in the form of film history (Lang and Eisenstein get replaced by Fellini and Kurosawa), it also lets us know that the illusion (because films are illusions) that we will one day figure it all out is itself a part of history, part of an ever changing but essentially similar heritage of bewilderment. The secret to be learned is that either there is no learning of this secret, or, worse, that there is no secret to be learned. The many who are prevented from making it are, among others, those in Berryman/Henry's life who could not go on living (he was haunted by his father's and several friends' suicides) because they felt they could not figure out the secret to living. The fact that Berryman himself committed suicide later in life makes it all even *more* meaningful to me; the simple evidence of someone trying to figure out life, someone trying so hard in so many different forms to say something true, and *still* not making it, touches me. The stupid, pathetic quality of Berryman's suicide makes the poem that much more intelligent and profound, and what makes the poem's intelligence and profundity stupid and pathetic is that these qualities weren't enough to save anyone's life.

I have been trying desperately since childhood to *figure it out*, and the yellow house was, I thought, a sign. As a child, I thought it was a sign that there was a grown-up life I would one day inhabit, a life essentially different from the one I inhabited as a child by virtue of the fact that I might understand and control my own life. As a young adult, starting symbolically from the day I saw the yellow house slide down that hole, I thought understanding life was about seeing it through art, about taking all those details I'd been hoarding and using them to my advantage; I thought I could *shape* my life, put it into a form. I thought the coincidence of seeing the yellow house hit by that wrecking ball meant that I was supposed to go and search for even more moments of truth, that I had to go out and actively seek such moments. I thought the moment with the house was special and profound and that I was special for having been privy to it. What I didn't understand was that such moments are happening all the time – *all* the time – and that what are rare are the moments when we are paying attention. There are no special significant moments of truth that can be isolated from other moments; each moment *is* the secret. We know the secret of being alive by being alive.

To this day I don't know the proper name of the material my green house was built out of, though I suppose I could find out if I really tried. For some reason I think about it more often than I used to, but I'm not convinced this means I care more. I still, however, think about those fake shutters, especially because the more I look, the more I see they are endemic to suburbs around the entire country, not just my childhood neighborhood. So contrived, so fake, so *dumb* those shutters always seemed to me. One day when I was eight or nine my perception altered slightly when a neighbor took his shutters down for some repair work on the house's siding. Their house, now shutterless, looked naked, somehow helpless. I remember standing there, startled by how, once the lie of the shutters was gone, the house looked even more like a lie, less and less like a home. Suddenly the house was just a box, not a place in which anyone would want to live. Yet, and this never failed to amaze me, people *did* live there, people I knew. No one lived in the yellow house except me, knocking around with the ghost of my invented life. How does my life now, my actual life as well as my written-about life, compare with the life I lived in that yellow house, or with that other life I lived in an oddly built green house in a neighborhood filled with fake shutters? What kind of storms did we think those shutters would keep out?

A NOTE ON THE AUTHOR

Lucy Grealy is an award-winning poet and author of the highly acclaimed memoir *Autobiography of a Face* (*New York Times* Notable Book of the Year). She lives in New York City and is currently working on a novel.

A NOTE ON THE TYPE

The text of this book is set in Linotype Sabon, named after the type founder, Jacques Sabon. It was designed by Jan Tschichold and jointly developed by Linotype, Monotype and Stempel, in response to a need for a typeface to be available in identical form for mechanical hot metal composition and hand composition using foundry type.

Tschichold based his design for Sabon roman on a fount engraved by Garamond, and Sabon italic on a fount by Granjon. It was first used in 1966 and has proved an enduring modern classic.